ARCHITECT REGISTRATION EXAM

CONSTRUCTION DOCUMENTS & SERVICES

ARE SAMPLE PROBLEMS AND PRACTICE EXAM

HOLLY WILLIAMS LEPPO, RA/CID
DAVID KENT BALLAST, FAIA

PPi The Power to Pass
www.ppi2pass.com

Professional Publications, Inc. • Belmont, California

How to Locate and Report Errata for This Book

At PPI, we do our best to bring you error-free books. But when errors do occur, we want to make sure you can view corrections and report any potential errors you find, so the errors cause as little confusion as possible.

A current list of known errata and other updates for this book is available on the PPI website at **www.ppi2pass.com/errata**. We update the errata page as often as necessary, so check in regularly. You will also find instructions for submitting suspected errata. We are grateful to every reader who takes the time to help us improve the quality of our books by pointing out an error.

CONSTRUCTION DOCUMENTS & SERVICES: ARE SAMPLE PROBLEMS AND PRACTICE EXAM

Current printing of this edition: 3

Printing History

edition number	printing number	update
1	1	New book.
1	2	Minor corrections.
1	3	Minor corrections.

Printed in the United States of America

PPI
1250 Fifth Avenue, Belmont, CA 94002
(650) 593-9119
www.ppi2pass.com

ISBN: 978-1-59126-123-0

TABLE OF CONTENTS

PREFACE AND ACKNOWLEDGMENTS

This book is tailored to the needs of those studying for version 4.0 of the Architect Registration Examination. The ARE 4.0 is one step in a process of change that began in 2001, when the National Council of Architectural Registration Boards (NCARB) published the results of a two-year study of the architecture profession. Since then, in response to that study, NCARB has introduced a series of changes to the ARE. Previous versions of the ARE have reduced the number of graphic vignettes and introduced new types of questions. Version 4.0, though, is the most substantial change yet, reorganizing and reducing the number of divisions and integrating graphic vignettes into divisions that were previously multiple choice only.

In the ARE 4.0, NCARB has eliminated the graphics-only Building Technology division and redistributed its six graphic vignettes into other divisions, combining them with multiple-choice sections of the exam. Each multiple-choice section carried over from version 3.1 now contains fewer questions, and a multiple-choice section has been added to the Site Planning & Design division (formerly called just Site Planning). The two structural divisions from version 3.1, General Structures and Lateral Forces, are now combined into one division, Structural Systems. In all, there are now seven divisions instead of nine, and there are somewhat fewer multiple-choice questions in all on the ARE 4.0 than on version 3.1.

In response to the version 4.0 changes, PPI has reorganized and revised its ARE review books. *ARE Review Manual* now covers all the divisions of the ARE in a single volume. This new book, *Construction Documents & Services: ARE Sample Problems and Practice Exam*, is one of seven companion volumes, one for each ARE 4.0 division. We believe that this organization will help you study for individual divisions most effectively.

You will find that this book and the related volumes are valuable parts of your exam preparation. Although there is no substitute for a good formal education and the broad-based experience provided by your internship with a practicing architect, this review series will help direct your study efforts to increase your chances of passing the ARE.

Many people have helped in the production of this book. We would like to thank all the fine people at PPI including Scott Marley (project editor), Amy Schwertman (typesetter, cover designer, and illustrator), and Thomas Bergstrom (illustrator).

Holly Williams Leppo, RA/CID

David Kent Ballast, FAIA

INTRODUCTION

ABOUT THIS BOOK

Construction Documents & Services: ARE Sample Problems and Practice Exam is written to help you prepare for the Construction Documents & Services division of the Architect Registration Examination (ARE), version 4.0.

Although this book can be a valuable study aid by itself, it is designed to be used along with the *ARE Review Manual*, also published by PPI. The *ARE Review Manual* is organized into sections that cover all seven divisions of the ARE 4.0.

- Programming, Planning & Practice
- Site Planning & Design
- Schematic Design
- Structural Systems
- Building Systems
- Building Design & Construction Systems
- Construction Documents & Services

This book is one of seven companion volumes to the *ARE Review Manual* that PPI publishes. Each of these books contains sample problems and practice exams for one of the ARE 4.0 divisions.

- *Programming, Planning & Practice: ARE Sample Problems and Practice Exam*
- *Site Planning & Design: ARE Sample Problems and Practice Exam*
- *Schematic Design: ARE Sample Problems and Practice Exam*
- *Structural Systems: ARE Sample Problems and Practice Exam*
- *Building Systems: ARE Sample Problems and Practice Exam*
- *Building Design & Construction Systems: ARE Sample Problems and Practice Exam*
- *Construction Documents & Services: ARE Sample Problems and Practice Exam*

THE ARCHITECT REGISTRATION EXAMINATION

Congratulations on completing (or nearing the end of) the Intern Development Program! You are two-thirds of the way to being able to call yourself an architect. NAAB degree? Check. IDP? Check. Now on to step three.

The final hurdle is the Architect Registration Examination. The ARE is a uniform test administered to candidates who wish to become licensed architects after they have served their required internships. It is given in all fifty states, all ten Canadian provinces, and five other jurisdictions including the District of Columbia, Guam, the Northern Mariana Islands, Puerto Rico, and the Virgin Islands.

The ARE has been developed to protect the health, safety, and welfare of the public by testing a candidate's entry-level competence to practice architecture. Its content relates as closely as possible to situations encountered in practice. It tests for the kinds of knowledge, skills, and abilities required of an entry-level architect, with particular emphasis on those services that affect public health, safety, and welfare. In order to accomplish these objectives, the exam tests for

- knowledge in specific subject areas
- the ability to make decisions
- the ability to consolidate and use information to solve a problem
- the ability to coordinate the activities of others on the building team

The ARE also includes some professional practice and project management questions.

The ARE is developed jointly by the National Council of Architectural Registration Boards (NCARB) and the Committee of Canadian Architectural Councils (CCAC), with the assistance of the Chauncey Group International and Prometric. The Chauncey Group serves as NCARB's test development and operations consultant, and Prometric operates and maintains the test centers where the ARE is administered.

Although the responsibility of professional licensing rests with each individual state, every state's board requires successful completion of the ARE to achieve registration or licensure. One of the primary reasons for a uniform test is to facilitate reciprocity—that is, to enable an architect to more easily gain a license to practice in states other than the one in which he or she was originally licensed.

The ARE is administered and graded entirely by computer. All divisions of the exam are offered six days a week at a network of test centers across North America. The results are scored by computer, and the results are forwarded to individual state boards of architecture, which process them and send them to candidates. If you fail a division, you must wait six months before you can retake that division.

First Steps

As you begin to prepare for the exam, you should first obtain a current copy of *ARE Guidelines* from NCARB. This booklet will get you started with the exam process and will be a valuable reference throughout. It includes descriptions of the seven divisions, instructions on how to apply, pay for, and take the ARE, and other useful information. You can download a PDF version at www.ncarb.org, or you can request a printed copy through the contact information provided at that site.

The NCARB website also gives current information about the exam, education requirements, training, examination procedures, and NCARB reciprocity services. It includes sample scenarios of the computer-based examination process and examples of costs associated with taking the computer-based exam.

The PPI website is also a good source of exam info (at **www.ppi2pass.com/areinfo**) and answers to frequently asked questions (at **www.ppi2pass.com/arefaq**).

To register as an examinee, you should obtain the registration requirements from the board in the state, province, or territory where you want to be registered. The exact requirements vary from one jurisdiction to another, so contact your local board. Links to state boards can be found at **www.ppi2pass.com/areinfo**.

As soon as NCARB has verified your qualifications and you have received your "Authorization to Test" letter, you may begin scheduling examinations. The exams are offered on a first come, first served basis and must be scheduled at least 72 hours in advance. See *ARE Guidelines* for instructions on finding a current list of testing centers. You may take the exams at any location, even outside the state in which you intend to become registered.

You may schedule any division of the ARE at any time and may take the divisions in any order. Divisions can be taken one at a time, to spread out preparation time and exam costs, or can be taken together in any combination.

However, each candidate must pass all seven divisions of the ARE within a single five-year period. This period, or "rolling clock," begins on the date of the first division you passed. If you have not completed the ARE within five years, the divisions that you passed more than five years ago are no longer credited, and the content in them must be retaken. Your new five-year period begins on the date of the earliest division you passed within the last five years.

About the ARE 4.0

NCARB's introduction of ARE version 4.0 in July 2008 marked the change to an exam format with both multiple-choice and graphic subjects appearing within the same division. In the previous version, the ARE 3.1, each division contained either multiple-choice problems or graphic problems, never both.

The ARE 4.0 also has fewer divisions than the ARE 3.1, seven instead of nine. The organization of the ARE 4.0 exam means that candidates will make fewer trips to the test center, and can study for related portions of the exam all at once.

Examination Format

The ARE 4.0 is organized into seven divisions that test various areas of architectural knowledge and problem-solving ability.

Programming, Planning & Practice

> 85 multiple-choice questions
> 1 graphic vignette: Site Zoning

Site Planning & Design

> 65 multiple-choice questions
> 2 graphic vignettes: Site Design, Site Grading

Schematic Design

> 2 graphic vignettes: Building Layout, Interior Layout

Structural Systems

> 125 multiple-choice questions
> 1 graphic vignette: Structural Layout

Building Systems

> 95 multiple-choice questions
> 1 graphic vignette: Mechanical & Electrical Plan

Building Design & Construction Systems

> 85 multiple-choice questions
> 3 graphic vignettes: Accessibility/Ramp, Roof Plan, Stair Design

Construction Documents & Services

> 100 multiple-choice questions
> 1 graphic vignette: Building Section

Experienced test-takers will tell you that there is quite a bit of overlap among these divisions. Questions that seem better suited to the Construction Documents & Services division may show up on the Building Design & Construction Systems division, for example, and questions on architectural history and building regulations might show up anywhere. That's why it's important to have a comprehensive strategy for studying and taking the exams.

The ARE is given entirely by computer. There are two kinds of problems on the exam. Multiple-choice problems are short questions presented on the computer screen; you answer them by clicking on the right answer or answers, or by filling in a blank. Graphic vignettes are longer problems in design; you solve a vignette by planning and drawing your solution on the computer. Six of the seven divisions contain both multiple-choice sections and graphic vignettes; the Schematic Design division contains only vignettes. Both kinds of problems are described later in this Introduction.

STUDY GUIDELINES

After the five to seven years (or even more) of higher education you've received to this point, you probably have a good idea of the study strategy that works best for you. The trick is figuring out how to apply that to the ARE. Unlike many college courses, there isn't a textbook or set of class notes from which all the exam questions will be derived. The exams are very broad and draw questions from multiple areas of knowledge.

The first challenge, then, is figuring out what to study. The ARE is never quite the same exam twice. The field of knowledge tested is always the same, but the specific questions asked are drawn randomly from a large pool, and will differ from one candidate to the next. One division may contain many code-related questions for one candidate and only a few for the next. This makes the ARE a challenge to study for.

ARE Guidelines contains lists of resources recommended by NCARB. That list can seem overwhelming, though, and on top of that, many of the recommended books are expensive or no longer in print. To help address this problem, a number of publishers sell study guides for the ARE. These guides summarize the information found in primary sources such as the NCARB-recommended books. A list of helpful resources for preparing for the Construction Documents & Services division can also be found in the Recommended Reading section of this book.

Your method of studying for the ARE should be based on both the content and form of the exam and on your school and work experience. Because the exam covers such a broad range of subject matter, it cannot possibly include every detail of practice. Rather, it tends to focus on what is considered entry-level knowledge and knowledge that is important for the protection of the public's health, safety, and welfare. Other types of questions are asked, too, but this knowledge should be the focus of your review schedule.

Your recent work experience should also help you determine what areas to study the most. A candidate who has been involved with construction documents for several years will probably need less review in that area than in others he or she has not had recent experience with.

The *ARE Review Manual* and its companion volumes are structured to help candidates focus on the topics that are more likely to be included in the exam in one form or another. Some subjects may seem familiar or may be easy to recall from memory, and others may seem completely foreign; the latter are the ones to give particular attention to. It may be wise to study additional sources on these subjects, take review seminars, or get special help from someone who is knowledgeable in the topic.

A typical candidate might spend about forty hours preparing for and taking each exam. Some will need to study more, some less. Forty hours is about one week of studying eight hours a day, or two weeks of four hours a day, or a month of two hours a day, along with reasonable breaks and time to attend to other responsibilities. As you probably work full time and have other family and personal obligations, it is important to develop a realistic schedule and do your best to stick to it. The ARE is not the kind of exam you can cram for the night before.

Also, since the fees are high and retaking a test is expensive, you want to do your best and pass in as few tries as possible. Allowing enough time to study and going into each exam well prepared will help you relax and concentrate on the questions.

The following steps may provide a useful structure for an exam study program.

Step 1: Start early. You can't review for a test like this by starting two weeks before the date. This is especially true if you are taking all portions of the exam for the first time.

Step 2: Go through the *ARE Review Manual* quickly to get a feeling for the scope of the subject matter and how the major topics are organized. Whatever division you're studying for, plan to review the chapters on building regulations as well. Review *ARE Guidelines*.

Step 3: Based on your review of the *ARE Review Manual* and *ARE Guidelines*, and on a realistic appraisal of your strong and weak areas, set priorities for study and determine which topics need more study time.

Step 4: Divide review subjects into manageable units and organize them into a sequence of study. It is generally best to start with the less familiar subjects. Based on the exam date and plans for beginning study, assign a time limit to each study unit. Again, your knowledge of a subject should determine the time devoted to it. You may want to devote an entire week to earthquake design if it is an unfamiliar subject, and only one day to timber design if it is a familiar one. In setting up a schedule, be realistic about other life commitments as well as your personal ability to concentrate on studying over a length of time.

Step 5: Begin studying, and stick with the schedule. Of course, this is the most difficult part of the process and the one that requires the most self-discipline. The job should be easier if you have started early and if you are following a realistic schedule that allows time for recreation and personal commitments.

Step 6: Stop studying a day or two before the exam. Relax. By this time, no amount of additional cramming will help.

At some point in your studying, you will want to spend some time becoming familiar with the program you will be using to solve the graphic vignettes, which does not resemble commercial CAD software. The software and sample vignettes can be downloaded from the NCARB website at www.ncarb.org.

There are many schools of thought on the best order for taking the divisions. One factor to consider is the six-month waiting period before you can retake a particular division. It's never fun to predict what you might fail, but if you know that a specific area might give you trouble, consider taking that exam near the beginning. You might be pleasantly surprised when you check the mailbox, but if not, as you work through the rest of the exams, the clock will be ticking and you can schedule the retest six months later.

Here are some additional tips.

- Learn concepts first, and then details later. For example, it is much better to understand the basic ideas and theories of waterproofing than it is to attempt to memorize dozens of waterproofing products and details. Once the concept is clear, the details are much easier to learn and to apply during the exam.

- Use the index to the *ARE Review Manual* to focus on particular subjects in which you feel weak, especially subjects that can apply to more than one division.

- Don't tackle all your hardest subjects first. Make one of your early exams one that you feel fairly confident about. It's nice to get off on the right foot with a PASS.

- Programming, Planning & Practice and Building Design & Construction Systems both tend to be "catch-all" divisions that cover a lot of material from the Construction Documents & Services division as well as others. Consider taking Construction Documents & Services first among those three, and then the other two soon after.

- Many past candidates recommend taking the Programming, Planning & Practice division last or nearly last, so that you will be familiar with the body of knowledge for all the other divisions as well.

- Brush up on architectural history before taking any of the divisions with multiple-choice sections. Know major buildings and their architects, particularly structures that are representative of an architect's philosophy (for example, Le Corbusier and the Villa Savoye) or that represent "firsts" or "turning points."

- Try to schedule your exams so that you'll have enough time to get yourself ready, eat, and review a little. If you'll have a long drive to the testing center, try to avoid having to make it during rush hour.

- If you are planning to take more than one division at a time, do not overstudy any one portion of the exam. It is generally better to review the concepts than to try to become an overnight expert in one area. For example, the exam may ask general questions about plate girders, but it will not ask for a complete, detailed design of a plate girder.

- Solve as many sample problems as possible, including those provided with NCARB's practice program, the books of sample problems and practice exams published by PPI, and any others that are available.

- Take advantage of the community of intern architects going through this experience with you. Some local AIA chapters offer ARE preparation courses or may be able to help you organize a study group with other interns in your area. Visit website forums to discuss the exam with others who have taken it or are preparing to take it. The Architecture Exam Forum at **www.ppi2pass.com/areforum** is a great online resource for questions, study advice, and encouragement. Even though the ARE questions change daily, it is a good idea to get a feeling for the types of questions that are being asked, the general emphasis, and the subject areas that previous candidates have found particularly troublesome.

- A day or two before the first test session, stop studying in order to relax as much as possible. Get plenty of sleep the night before the test.

- Try to relax as much as possible during study periods and during the exam itself. Worrying is counterproductive. Candidates who have worked diligently in school, have obtained a wide range of experience during internship, and have started exam review early will be in the best possible position to pass the ARE.

TAKING THE EXAM

What to Bring

Bring multiple forms of photo ID and your Authorization to Test letter to the test site.

It is neither necessary nor permitted to bring any reference materials or scratch paper into the test site. Pencils and scratch paper are provided by the proctor and must be returned when leaving the exam room. Earplugs will also be provided. Leave all your books and notes in the car. Most testing centers have lockers for your keys, small personal belongings, and cell phone.

Do not bring a calculator into the test site. A calculator built into the testing software will be available in all divisions.

Arriving at the Testing Center

Allow plenty of time to get to the exam site, to avoid transportation problems such as getting lost or stuck in traffic jams. If you can, arrive a little early, and take a little time in the parking lot to review one last time the formulas and

other things you need to memorize. Then relax, take a few deep breaths, and go take the exam.

Once at the testing center, you will check in with the attendant, who will verify your identification and your Authorization to Test. (Don't forget to take this home with you after each exam; you'll need it for the next one.) After you check in, you'll be shown to your testing station.

When the exam begins, you will have the opportunity to click through a tutorial that explains how the computer program works. You'll probably want to read through it the first time, but after that initial exam, you will know how the software works and you won't need the tutorial. Take a deep breath, organize your paper and pencils, and take advantage of the opportunity to dump all the facts floating around in your brain onto your scratch paper—write down as much as you can. This includes formulas, ratios ("if x increases, y decreases"), and so on—anything that you are trying desperately not to forget. If you can get all the things you've crammed at the last minute onto that paper, you'll be able to think a little more clearly about the questions posed on the screen.

Taking the Multiple-Choice Sections

The ARE multiple-choice sections include several types of questions.

One type of multiple-choice question is based on written, graphic, or photographic information. The candidate examines the information and selects the correct answer from four given answer choices. Some problems may require calculations.

A second type of multiple-choice question lists four or five items or statements, which are given Roman numerals from I to IV or I to V. For example, the question may give five statements about a subject, and the candidate must choose the statements that are true. The four answer choices are combinations of these numerals, such as "I and III" or "II, IV, and V".

A third type of multiple-choice question describes a situation that could be encountered in actual practice. Drawings, diagrams, photographs, forms, tables, or other data may also be given. The question asks the examinee to select the best answer from four options.

Two kinds of questions that NCARB calls "alternate item types" also show up in the multiple-choice sections. In a "fill in the blank" question, the examinee must fill a blank with a number derived from a table or calculation. In a "check all that apply" question, six answer choices are given, and the candidate must choose all the correct answers. The question tells how many of the choices are correct, from two to four.

The examinee must choose all the correct answers to receive credit; partial credit is not given.

Between 10% and 15% of the questions in a multiple-choice section will be these "alternate item type" questions. Every question on the ARE, however, counts the same toward your total score.

Keep in mind that multiple-choice questions often require the examinee to do more than just select an answer based on memory. At times it will be necessary to combine several facts, analyze data, perform a calculation, or review a drawing. Remember, too, that most candidates do not need the entire time allotted for the multiple-choice sections. If you have time for more than one pass through the questions, you can make good use of it.

Here are some tips for the multiple-choice problems.

- Go through the entire section in one somewhat swift pass, answering the questions that you're sure about and marking the others so you can return to them later. If a question requires calculations, skip it for now unless it's very simple. Then go back to the beginning and work your way through the exam again, taking a little more time to read each question and think through the answer.

- Another benefit of going through the entire section at the beginning is that occasionally there is information in one question that may help you answer another question somewhere else.

- If you are very unsure of a question, pick your best answer choice, mark it, and move on. You will probably have time at the end of the test to go back and recheck these answers. But remember, your first response is usually the best.

- Always answer all the questions. Unanswered questions are counted wrong, so even if you are just guessing, it's better to choose an answer and have a chance of it being correct than to skip it and be certain of getting it wrong. When faced with four answer choices, the old SAT strategy of eliminating the two answers that are definitely wrong and making your best guess between the two that remain is helpful on the ARE, too.

- Some questions may seem too simple. Although a few very easy and obvious questions are included on the ARE, more often the simplicity should serve as a red flag to warn you to reevaluate the question for exceptions to a rule or special circumstances that make the obvious, easy response incorrect.

- Watch out for absolute words in a question, such as "always," "never," and "completely." These are often a clue that some little exception exists, turning what reads like a true statement into a false one or vice versa.

- Be alert for words like "seldom," "usually," "best," and "most reasonable." These indicate that some judgment will be involved in answering the question. Look for two or more options that appear to be very similar.

- Some divisions will provide an on-screen reference sheet with useful formulas and other information that will help you solve some problems. Skim through the reference sheet so you know what information is there, and then use it as a resource.

- Occasionally there may be a defective question. This does not happen very often, but if it does, make the best choice possible under the circumstances. Flawed questions are usually discovered, and either they are not counted on the test or any one of the correct answers is credited.

Solving the Vignettes

Each of the eleven graphic vignettes on the ARE is designed to test a particular area of knowledge and skill. Each one presents a base plan of some kind and gives programmatic and other requirements. The candidate must create a plan that satisfies the requirements.

In the *Building Section* vignette, the candidate must develop a schematic section of a two-story building, given the partial floor plans where the section is cut. Information is given about building materials, structural systems, frost depth, mechanical systems, and heights and elevations of some elements. The candidate must show how structural elements, mechanical systems, and space for lighting are integrated into the solution, and indicate appropriate footing and foundation depths and sizes, bearing walls, beams, and correct thicknesses for the given floor and roof assemblies. Parapets must be shown. Rated assemblies may be part of the problem.

The computer scores the vignettes by a complex grading method. Design criteria are given various point values, and responses are categorized as Acceptable, Unacceptable, or Indeterminate.

General Tips for the Vignettes

Here are some general tips for approaching the vignettes. More detailed solving tips can be found in the chapter in this book that covers each vignette.

- Remember that with the current format and computer grading, each vignette covers only a very specific area of knowledge and offers a limited number of possible solutions. In a few cases only one solution is really possible. Use this as an advantage.

- Read the problem thoroughly, twice. Follow the requirements exactly, letting each problem solve itself as much as possible. Be careful not to read more into the problem than is there. The test writers are very specific about what they want; there is no need to add to the problem requirements. If a particular type of solution is strongly suggested, follow that lead.

- Consider only those code requirements given in the vignette, even if they deviate from familiar codes. Do not read anything more into the problem. The code requirements may be slightly different from what candidates use in practice.

- Use the scratch paper provided to sketch possible solutions before starting the final solution.

- Make sure all programmed elements are included in the final design.

- When the functional requirements of the problem have been solved, use the problem statement as a checklist to make sure all criteria have been satisfied.

General Tips for Using the Vignette Software

It is important to practice with the vignette software that will be used in the exam. The program is unique to the ARE and unlike standard CAD software. If you are unfamiliar with the software interface you will waste valuable time learning to use it, and are likely to run out of time before completing the vignettes. Practice software can be downloaded at no charge from NCARB's website at www.ncarb.org. Usage time for the practice program can also be purchased at Prometric test centers. The practice software includes tutorials, directions, and one practice vignette for each of the eleven vignettes.

Here are some general tips for using the vignette software.

- When elements overlap on the screen, it may be difficult to select a particular element. If this happens, repeatedly click on the element without moving the mouse until the desired element is highlighted.

- Try to stay in "ortho" mode. This mode can be used to solve most problems, and it makes the solution process much easier and quicker. Unless obviously required by the vignette, creating additional angles complicates any problem with the time restrictions given.

- If the vignette relates to contour modifications, it may help to draw schematic sections through the significant existing slopes. This provides a three-dimensional image of the problem.

- When drawing, if the program states that elements should connect, make sure they touch at their boundaries only and do not overlap. Use the *check* tool to determine if there are any overlaps. Walls that do not align correctly can cause a solution to be downgraded or even rejected. Remember, walls between spaces change color temporarily when properly aligned.

- Make liberal use of the *zoom* tool for sizing and aligning components accurately. Zoom in as closely as possible on the area being worked. When aligning objects, it is also helpful to use the full-screen cursor.

- Turn on the grid and verify spacing. This makes it easier to align objects and get a sense of the sizes of objects and the distances between them. Use the *measure* tool to check exact measurements if needed.

- Make liberal use of the sketch tools. These can be turned on and off and do not count during the grading, but they can be used to show relationships and for temporary guidelines and other notations.

- Use sketch circles to show required distances, setbacks, clearances, and similar measures.

AFTER THE EXAM

When you've clicked the button to end the test, the computer may prompt you to provide some demographic information about yourself and your education and experience. Then gather your belongings, turn in your scratch paper and materials—you must leave them with the proctor—and leave the testing center. (For security reasons, you can't remove anything from the test center.) If the staff has retained your Authorization to Test and your identification, don't forget to retrieve both.

If you should encounter any problems during the exams or have any concerns, be sure to report them to the test center administrator and to NCARB as soon as possible. If you wait longer than ten days after you test, NCARB will not respond to your complaint. You must report your complaint immediately and directly to NCARB and copy your state registration board for any hope of assistance.

Then it's all over but the wait for the mail. How long it takes to get your scores will vary with the efficiency of your state registration board, which reviews the scores from NCARB before passing along the results. But four to six weeks is typical.

As you may have heard from classmates and colleagues, the ARE is a difficult exam—but it is certainly not impossible to pass. A solid architectural education and a well-rounded internship are the best preparation you can have. Watch carefully and listen to the vocabulary used by architects with more experience. Look for opportunities to participate in all phases of project delivery so that you have some "real world" experience to apply to the scenarios you will inevitably find in exam questions.

One last piece of advice is not to put off taking the exams. Take them as soon as you become eligible. You will probably still remember a little bit from your college courses and you may even have your old textbooks and notes handy. As life gets more complicated—with spouses and children and work obligations—it is easy to make excuses and never find time to get around to it. Make the commitment, and do it now. After all, this is the last step to reaching your goal of calling yourself an architect.

HOW TO USE THIS BOOK

This book contains 128 sample multiple-choice problems and one sample vignette, as well as one complete practice exam consisting of 100 multiple-choice problems and one vignette. These have been written to help you prepare for the Construction Documents & Services division of the Architect Registration Examination, version 4.0.

One of the best ways to prepare for the ARE is by solving sample problems. While you are studying for this division, use the sample problems in this book to make yourself familiar with the different types of questions and the breadth of topics you are likely to encounter on the actual exam. Then when it's time to take the ARE, you will already be comfortable with the format of the exam questions. Also, seeing which sample problems you can and cannot answer correctly will help you gauge your understanding of the topics covered in the Construction Documents & Services division.

The sample multiple-choice problems in this book are organized by subject area, so that you can concentrate on one subject at a time if you like. Each problem is immediately followed by its answer and an explanation.

The sample vignette in this book can be solved directly on the base plan provided or on a sheet of tracing paper. Alternatively, you can download an electronic file of the base plan in PDF format from **www.ppi2pass.com/vignettes** for use in your own CAD program. (On the actual exam, vignettes are solved on the computer using NCARB's own software; see the Introduction for more information about this.) When you are finished with your solution to the vignette, compare it against the sample passing and failing solutions that follow.

While the sample problems in this book are intended for you to use as you study for the exam, the practice exam is best used only when you have almost finished your study of the Construction Documents & Services topics. A week or two before you are scheduled to take the division, when you feel you are nearly ready for the exam, do a "dry run" by taking the practice exam in this book. This will hone your test-taking skills and give you a reality check about how prepared you really are.

The experience will be most valuable to you if you treat the practice exam as though it were an actual exam. Do not read the questions ahead of time and do not look at the solutions until after you've finished. Try to simulate the exam experience as closely as possible. This means locking yourself away in a quiet space, setting an alarm for the exam's testing time, and working through the entire examination with no coffee, television, or telephone—only your calculator, a pencil, your drafting tools or CAD program for the vignette, and a few sheets of scratch paper. (On the actual exam, these are provided.) This will help you prepare to budget your time, give you an idea of what the actual exam experience will be like, and help you develop a test-taking strategy that works for you.

The target times for the sections of the practice exam are

Multiple choice: 2 hours

Building Section vignette: 1 hour

Record your answers for the multiple-choice section of the practice exam using the "bubble" answer form at the front of the exam. When you are finished, you can check your answers quickly against the filled-in answer key at the front of the Solutions section. Then turn to the solutions and read the explanations of the answers, especially those you answered incorrectly. The explanation will give you a better understanding of the intent of the question and why individual choices are right or wrong.

The Solutions section may also be used as a guide for the final phase of your studies. As opposed to a traditional study guide that is organized into chapters and paragraphs of facts, this question-and-answer format can help you see how the exam might address a topic, and what types of questions you are likely to encounter. If you still are not clear about a particular subject after reading a solution's explanation, review the subject in one of your study resources. Give yourself time for further study, and then take the multiple-choice section again.

The vignette portion of the practice exam can be solved the same way as the sample vignette, either directly on the base plans, on tracing paper, or with a CAD program using the electronic files downloaded from **www.ppi2pass.com/vignettes**. Try to solve each vignette within the target time given. When you are finished, compare your drawing against the passing and failing solutions given in the Solutions section.

This book is best used in conjunction with your primary study source or study guide, such as PPI's *ARE Review Manual. Construction Documents & Services: ARE Sample Problems and Practice Exam* is not intended to give you all the information you will need to pass this division of the ARE. Rather, it is designed to expose you to a variety of problem types and to help you sharpen your problem-solving and test-taking skills. With a sound review and the practice you'll get from this book, you'll be well on your way to successfully passing the Construction Documents & Services division of the Architect Registration Examination.

HOW SI UNITS ARE USED IN THIS BOOK

This book includes equivalent measurements in the text and illustrations using the Système International (SI), or the metric system as it is commonly called. However, the use of SI units for construction and book publishing in the United States is problematic. This is because the building construction industry in the United States (with the exception of federal construction) has generally not adopted the metric system. As a result, equivalent measurements of customary U.S. units (also called English or inch-pound units) are usually given as a *soft* conversion, in which customary U.S. measurements are simply converted into SI units using standard conversion factors. This always results in a number with excessive significant digits. When construction is done using SI units, the building is designed and drawn according to *hard* conversions, where planning dimensions and building products are based on a metric module from the beginning. For example, studs are spaced 400 mm on center to accommodate panel products that are manufactured in standard 1200 mm widths.

During the present time of transition to the Système International in the United States, code-writing bodies, federal laws such as the ADA, product manufacturers, trade associations, and other construction-related industries typically still use the customary U.S. system and make soft conversions to develop SI equivalents. In the case of some product manufacturers, they produce the same product using both measuring systems. Although there are industry standards for developing SI equivalents, there is no perfect consistency for rounding off when conversions are made. For example, the International Building Code shows a 152 mm equivalent when a 6 in dimension is required, while the Americans with Disabilities Act Accessibility Guidelines (ADAAG) give a 150 mm equivalent for the same customary U.S. dimension.

To further complicate matters, each book publisher may employ a slightly different house style in handling SI equivalents when customary U.S. units are used as the primary measuring system. The confusion is likely to continue until the United States construction industry adopts the SI system completely, eliminating the need for dual dimensioning in publishing.

For the purposes of this book, the following conventions have been adopted.

Throughout the book, the customary U.S. measurements are given first with the SI equivalent shown in parentheses. When the measurement is millimeters, units are not shown. For example, a dimension may be indicated as 4 ft 8 in (1422). When the SI equivalent is some other unit, such as for volume or area, the units are indicated. For example, 250 ft^2 (23 m^2).

Following standard conventions, all SI distance measurements in illustrations are in millimeters unless specifically indicated as meters.

When a measurement is given as part of a problem scenario, the SI measurement is not necessarily meant to be roughly equal to the U.S. measurement. For example, a hypothetical force on a beam might be given as 12 kips (12 kN). 12 kips is actually equal to about 53.38 kN, but the intention in such cases is only to provide two problems, one in U.S. units and one in SI units, of about the same difficulty. Solve the entire problem in either U.S. or SI units; don't try to convert from one to the other in the middle of solving a problem.

When dimensions are for informational use, the SI equivalent rounded to the nearest millimeter is used.

When dimensions are given and they relate to planning or design guidelines, the SI equivalent is rounded to the nearest 5 mm for numbers over a few inches and to the nearest 10 mm for numbers over a few feet. When the dimension exceeds several feet, the number is rounded to the nearest 100 mm. For example, if you need a space about 10 ft wide for a given activity, the modular, rounded SI equivalent will be given as 3000 mm. More exact conversions are not required.

xviii   CONSTRUCTION DOCUMENTS & SERVICES

When an item is only manufactured to a customary U.S. measurement, the nearest SI equivalent rounded to the nearest millimeter is given, unless the dimension is very small (as for metal gages), in which case a more precise decimal equivalent will be given. Some materials, such as glass, are often manufactured to SI sizes. So, for example, a nominal $1/2$ in thick piece of glass will have an SI equivalent of 13 mm but can be ordered as 12 mm.

When there is a hard conversion in the industry and an SI equivalent item is manufactured, the hard conversion is given. For example, a 24 × 24 ceiling tile would have the hard conversion of 600 × 600 (instead of 610) because these are manufactured and available in the United States.

When an SI conversion is used by a code agency, such as the International Building Code (IBC), or published in another regulation, such as the ADA Accessibility Guidelines, the SI equivalents used by the issuing agency are printed in this book. For example, the same 10 ft dimension given previously as 3000 mm for a planning guideline would have an SI equivalent of 3048 mm in the context of the IBC because this is what that code requires. The ADA Accessibility Guidelines generally follow the rounding rule, to take SI dimensions to the nearest 10 mm. For example, a 10 ft requirement for accessibility will be shown as 3050 mm. The code requirements for readers outside the United States may be slightly different.

This book uses different abbreviations for pounds of force and pounds of mass in customary U.S. units. The abbreviation used for pounds of force (pounds-force) is lbf, and the abbreviation used for pounds of mass (pounds-mass) is lbm.

PROFESSIONAL PUBLICATIONS, INC.

CODES AND STANDARDS
USED IN THIS BOOK

American Institute of Architects. Contract Documents, 1997. Washington, DC.

Canadian Construction Documents Committee. CCDC Standard Documents, 2006. Ottawa.

RECOMMENDED READING

General Reference

Access Board. *ADAAG Manual: A Guide to the Americans with Disabilities Accessibility Guidelines.* East Providence, RI: BNI Building News.

_____. *ADAAG Manual: Americans with Disabilities Act Accessibility Guidelines for Buildings and Facilities.* Washington, DC: U.S. Architectural and Transportation Barriers Compliance Board. www.access-board.gov/adaag/html/adaag.htm.

ARCOM. *MASTERSPEC.* Salt Lake City: ARCOM. (Familiarity with the format and language of specifications is very helpful.)

ARCOM and American Institute of Architects. *The Graphic Standards Guide to Architectural Finishes: Using Masterspec® to Evaluate, Select, and Specify Materials.* New York: John Wiley & Sons.

Ballast, David Kent, and Steven O'Hara. *ARE Review Manual.* Belmont, CA: PPI.

Canadian Commission on Building and Fire Codes. *National Building Code of Canada.* Ottawa: National Research Council of Canada.

Fitch, James Marston. *Historic Preservation: Curatorial Management of the Built World.* Charlottesville: University Press of Virginia.

Guthrie, Pat. *Architect's Portable Handbook.* New York: McGraw-Hill.

Harris, Cyril M., ed. *Dictionary of Architecture and Construction.* New York: McGraw-Hill.

International Code Council. *International Building Code.* Washington, DC: International Code Council.

_____. *Standard on Accessible and Usable Buildings and Facilities* (ICC/ANSI A117.1). Washington, DC: American National Standards Institute, International Code Council.

Patterson, Terry L. *Illustrated 2000 Building Code Handbook.* New York: McGraw-Hill.

Ramsey, Charles G., and Harold R. Sleeper. *Architectural Graphic Standards.* New York: John Wiley & Sons. (The student edition is an acceptable substitute for the professional version.)

U.S. Green Building Council. *LEED Reference Package for New Construction and Major Renovations.* Washington, DC: U.S. Green Building Council.

Construction Documents & Services

American Institute of Architects. *AIA Documents* (especially A201 and B141). Washington, DC: American Institute of Architects. (The ARE 4.0 tests on the 1997 AIA documents. Download documents with commentary from www.aia.org/docs_free_paperdocuments.)

_____. *The Architect's Handbook of Professional Practice.* Washington, DC: The American Institute of Architects. (Includes AIA standard documents.)

Committee of Canadian Architectural Councils and The Royal Architectural Institute of Canada. *Canadian Handbook of Practice for Architects.* Royal Architectural Institute of Canada.

Construction Specifications Institute. *CSI Manual of Practice.* Alexandria, VA: The Construction Specifications Institute.

_____. *MasterFormat™.* Alexandria, VA: The Construction Specifications Institute.

_____. *The Uniform Drawing System.* Alexandria, VA: The Construction Specifications Institute.

Demkin, Joseph A., ed. *Architect's Handbook of Professional Practice* by The American Institute of Architects. New York: John Wiley & Sons. (The student edition is an acceptable substitute for the professional version.)

Liebing, Ralph. *Architectural Working Drawings*. New York: John Wiley & Sons.

National Council of Architectural Registration Boards. *Rules of Conduct*. Washington, DC: National Council of Architectural Registration Boards (Download from www.ncarb.org/Forms/roconduct.pdf.)

Rosen, Harold J. *Construction Specifications Writing: Principles and Procedures*. New York: John Wiley & Sons.

Sweet, Justin. *Legal Aspects of Architecture, Engineering, and the Construction Process*. Pacific Grove, CA: Brooks Cole.

Graphic Vignettes

Allen, Edward, and Joseph Iano. *The Architect's Studio Companion: Rules of Thumb for Preliminary Design*. New York: John Wiley & Sons.

Ambrose, James, and Peter Brandow. *Simplified Site Design*. New York: John Wiley & Sons.

Ching, Francis D. K., and Steven R. Winkel. *Building Codes Illustrated: A Guide to Understanding the International Building Code*. New York: John Wiley & Sons.

Hoke, John Ray, ed. *Architectural Graphic Standards*. New York: John Wiley & Sons.

Karlen, Mark. *Space Planning Basics*. New York: John Wiley & Sons.

Parker, Harry, John W. MacGuire, and James Ambrose. *Simplified Site Engineering*. New York: John Wiley & Sons.

Architectural History

(Brush up on this before taking any of the multiple-choice exams, as architectural history questions are scattered throughout the sections.)

Curtis, William J.R. *Modern Architecture Since 1900*. London: Phaedon Press, Ltd.

Frampton, Kenneth. *Modern Architecture: A Critical History*. London: Thames and Hudson.

Trachtenberg, Marvin, and Isabelle Hyman. *Architecture: From Pre-History to Post-Modernism*. Englewood Cliffs, NJ: Prentice-Hall.

SAMPLE PROBLEMS

CODES AND REGULATIONS

1. According to ADAAG, what is the minimum clear floor space for one stationary wheelchair?

    A. 24 in (610) by 36 in (915)
    B. 30 in (760) by 48 in (1220)
    C. 32 in (815) by 48 in (1220)
    D. 60 in (1525) by 60 in (1525)

Solution

The minimum clear floor space required for one stationary wheelchair is 30 in (760) by 48 in (1220) This critical dimension is the basis for many other accessibility guidelines, such as the amount of clear floor space required at a lavatory and the width of a hallway required to allow two wheelchairs to pass (60 in (1525), which is 30 in (760) times two).

The answer is B.

2. An assembly occupancy with an occupant load of fewer than 50 persons would be classified as occupancy group

    A. M
    B. E
    C. A
    D. B

Solution

An assembly occupancy with an occupant load of fewer than 50 persons would be considered a group B, or business, occupancy.

The answer is D.

3. Which of these events triggered revisions to the building codes?

    A. the Chicago Fire of 1871
    B. the San Francisco Earthquake and Fire of 1906
    C. the terrorist attacks of September 11, 2001
    D. all of the above

Solution

As constantly evolving documents, the building codes have undergone many revisions to reflect the introduction of new materials, building technologies, and challenges. The biggest changes to the codes tend to follow disasters, when the shortcomings of the previous requirements become apparent. All the events listed, plus many other natural and human-made disasters, have influenced the thinking behind the requirements of the codes with the intention of making buildings safer and protecting human life.

The answer is D.

4. Occupant load factors are calculated based upon

    A. the number of exits
    B. the net floor area
    C. the gross floor area
    D. the net or gross floor area, depending on the occupancy

Solution

Occupant load factors are calculated based upon either net or gross floor area, depending on the occupancy. The IBC refers to Table 1004.1 to determine which calculation is appropriate for a particular situation. The *occupant load* represents the number of people that the code assumes will occupy a space or building. This number is then used to determine egress requirements.

The answer is D.

5.   According to ADAAG, what is the maximum distance an object may protrude into the path of travel when it is mounted to a wall between 27 in (685) and 80 in (2030) above finish floor?

    A. 2 in (50)
    B. 4 in (100)
    C. 6 in (150)
    D. 8 in (205)

Solution

An object mounted to the wall between 27 in (685) and 80 in (2030) above finish floor may protrude a maximum of 4 in (100) into the path of travel. This requirement is intended to minimize obstructions that a person with impaired vision may possibly walk in to. Obstructions placed lower than 27 in (685) may project more than 4 in (100) as long as other requirements for access are maintained, because a person using a cane can detect the obstructions.

The answer is B.

6.   An office in an unsprinklered building has an occupant load of 290. Which of the following exit door combinations would minimally satisfy the exit width required?

    A. a pair of 30 in (762) entry doors and a 36 in (914) door remotely located
    B. two 36 in (914) doors on opposite sides of the building
    C. three 32 in (813) doors remotely located
    D. three 36 in (914) doors remotely located from each other

Solution

To find the total exit width required, multiply the occupant load, 290 people, by the standard 0.2 in/person (5 mm/person).

In U.S. units:

$$(290 \text{ people})(0.2 \text{ in/person}) = 58 \text{ in}$$

In SI units:

$$(290 \text{ people})(5 \text{ mm/person}) = 1450 \text{ mm}$$

Any exit door must provide a clear width of at least 32 in (813), so choices A and C cannot be correct because their clear widths would be less than 32 in (813). Three 36 in (914) doors would be acceptable, but the question asks for the minimally acceptable solution, which is two 36 in (914) doors; this would provide approximately 66 in (1676) of width (considering the clear width of the door to be from the doorstop to the face of the door when open).

The answer is B.

7.   Which of the following statements about standards and testing is FALSE?

    A. Trade association standards must be followed if they are referred to by a building code adopted in a jurisdiction.
    B. The American National Standards Institute (ANSI) does not write standards.
    C. The American Society for Testing and Materials (ASTM) does not perform tests.
    D. Building codes prescribe which laboratories must perform required tests.

Solution

Building codes only prescribe which tests and standards a material or construction element must meet in order to be acceptable. Any qualified Nationally Recognized Testing Laboratory (NRTL) may perform a test, as long as the lab follows the procedures described in the test.

The answer is D.

8. Measured vertically from the nosing of the stair, how high must a handrail be for barrier-free design?

    A. 28 in (711) to 32 in (815)
    B. 30 in (760) to 34 in (865)
    C. 32 in (815) to 36 in (915)
    D. 34 in (865) to 38 in (965)

Solution

For barrier-free design, a handrail must be 34 in (865) to 38 in (965) high, measured vertically from the nosing of the stair.

The answer is D.

9. An architect has been hired to prepare a design for remodeling toilet rooms to make them accessible. The architect finds it is impossible to provide adequate clearance on one side of an entrance door. What is the most economical course of action?

    A. Apply to the building department for a hardship exemption because compliance is not readily achievable.
    B. Tell the client that walls should be demolished and the toilet rooms replanned to provide the necessary clearances.
    C. Specify a power-assisted door opener that meets accessibility standards for the noncompliant door.
    D. Plan for accessible toilet rooms in another location in the building where all requirements can be adequately met.

Solution

A power-assisted door would be the least expensive option and require the least construction time. It would be possible to solve the problem by demolishing the existing restrooms and rebuilding them to comply with accessibility standards, or meet the requirement for accessible facilities in another location in the building, but both of these options are likely to be less economical than the door opener.

The answer is C.

10. Which of the following ramp configurations meets barrier-free design requirements?

    A. 1:14 slope with maximum rise of 24 in (610)
    B. 1:12 slope with maximum rise of 34 in (865)
    C. 1:10 slope with maximum rise of 8 in (203)
    D. 1:8 slope with maximum rise of 4 in (100)

Solution

The maximum acceptable slope for compliance with accessibility guidelines is 1:12, but the maximum total rise between landings is limited to 30 in (760). A 1:14 slope is less steep than 1:12 and the maximum rise of 24 in (610) given in choice A both comply with the guidelines. A 1:10 slope is allowed if the maximum rise is held to 6 in (150) or less. A 1:8 slope is permitted only if the maximum rise is 3 in (75) or less.

The answer is A.

11. In the diagram shown, what is the minimum distance, *x*, between two entry doors in the vestibule?

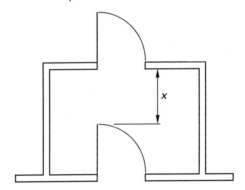

    A. 36 in (915)
    B. 42 in (1065)
    C. 48 in (1220)
    D. 60 in (1525)

Solution

The minimum distance between two entry doors forming a vestibule when one opens out and one opens in is 48 in (1220).

The answer is C.

CONSTRUCTION DRAWINGS

12. The element labeled *X* in this drawing of an interior windowsill is the

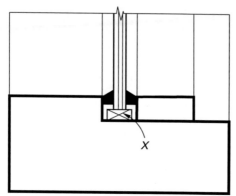

A. anti-walk block
B. glazing bead
C. setting block
D. removable stop

Solution

In all windowsill details, the glass is placed on two or more *setting blocks* to support the weight of the glass and cushion it from the frame.

Anti-walk blocks are sometimes used in jamb frames to prevent the glass from touching the jambs. A *glazing bead* describes a material used to cushion and seal the glass against the stop and the frame. A *stop* is a removable piece used to hold the glass in place after it has been installed in the frame, which makes it possible to replace the glass when necessary.

The answer is C.

13. In a full set of construction drawings, the mechanical engineering drawings are typically placed

A. after the civil engineering drawings and before the architectural drawings
B. immediately after the architectural drawings
C. after the structural engineering drawings and before the electrical drawings
D. after the electrical drawings

Solution

The normal sequence of drawings in a full set of drawings is as follows: site drawings, then civil engineering drawings, followed by architectural, structural, mechanical, plumbing (if not included in mechanical), and electrical drawings.

The answer is C.

14. Which of the following symbols indicates a floor telephone outlet?

A.

B.

C.

D.

Solution

A floor telephone outlet symbol is indicated in Option A.

Option B indicates a floor duplex electrical outlet. Option C is the symbol for a thermostat. Option D indicates a data outlet.

> *Study Note:* Be familiar with standard mechanical and electrical symbols as well as the appearance of architectural, structural, mechanical, and electrical floor plans and other types of drawings.

The answer is A.

15. During preparation of construction drawings, the architect should coordinate with the structural engineer by

A. requiring the engineer to submit progress drawings when changes are made
B. conducting weekly meetings with the engineer and exchanging progress copies of drawings
C. holding conference calls between staff at both offices at times required by the work progress
D. submitting weekly written memos to the engineer describing the architectural requirements

Solution

Two-way communication of graphic information is critical if the complex coordination required between consultants and the architect is to be successful. Regularly scheduled meetings and exchange of progress documents achieve this goal.

Submission of engineering progress drawings implies only a one-way exchange of information. Conference calls alone cannot fully describe the visual information being developed during production of construction documents. Telephone calls or emails must be supplemented with some type of exchange of visual information through computer networking, faxes, or a physical exchange of printed drawings. The written word is not sufficient to describe drawings, and tends to be a one-way method of communication.

The answer is B.

16.   While the architect is coordinating a set of construction documents, the interior designer submits the drawing shown.

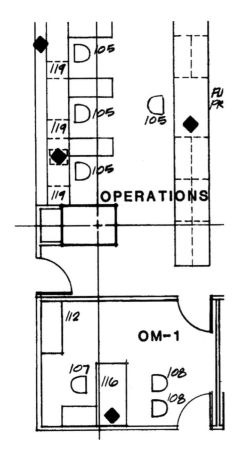

The drawing is a portion of

    A.   a finish plan
    B.   a furniture location plan
    C.   a telecommunications plan
    D.   an equipment layout

Solution

This partial drawing shows furniture locations and the individual pieces identified with numbers. It would be coordinated with a schedule that would specify each piece of furniture.

The answer is B.

Questions 17 and 18 refer to the accompanying Wall Detail at 2nd Floor.

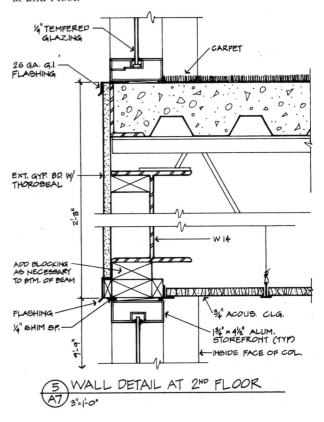

17.   If this detail is on an east-facing elevation in Boston, what change should the architect make?

    A.   Modify the drip detail at the top of the window frame.
    B.   Change the glazing.
    C.   Add seismic fasteners for the suspended ceiling.
    D.   Increase the shim space.

Solution

The most significant problem with this detail in a cold climate like that of Boston is the lack of insulated glazing. The detail only indicates a single pane of glass. Although the question does not address this issue, notice also that there is no insulation between the ceiling and the floor above.

The answer is B.

18. In the detail shown, which of the following would be of greatest concern?

    A. attachment of exterior materials to the structure

    B. possible water leakage

    C. lack of tolerance for the storefront system

    D. cracking from differential movement of materials

Solution

Water leakage is the greatest concern in this construction detail. Although flashing is shown and noted below the sill of the second-floor framing, extending it under the framing to the edge of the carpet is inadvisable. In addition, there is no sealant called out for the joint between the sill and the flashing. Water dripping down the window could be drawn into the framing by capillary action.

The answer is B.

19. The following symbols may appear on a consultant's drawings. In order, identify the disconnect switch, the diffuser, the home run to panel board, and the weld.

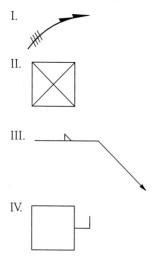

I.

II.

III.

IV.

    A. I, III, II, IV

    B. II, I, III, IV

    C. IV, III, II, I

    D. IV, II, I, III

The answer is D.

20. Who is responsible for verifying that recessed downlights do not interfere with the ductwork shown on the plans?

    A. architect

    B. electrical engineer

    C. lighting designer

    D. mechanical engineer

Solution

The architect is responsible for the overall coordination of all the contract documents prepared by his or her consultants.

The answer is A.

21. Plans, sections, and elevations are examples of

    A. isometric drawings

    B. axonometric drawings

    C. orthographic drawings

    D. oblique drawings

Solution

Plans, sections, and elevations are examples of *orthographic projections*. These drawings "project" the building onto a drawing surface parallel to the object. This allows the elements of the building to be shown to scale but eliminates depth from the drawing. Other drawing conventions, such as lineweight, must be used to communicate which parts of the building are closest to the viewer and which portions recede.

Axonometric drawings are prepared by rotating the plan at an angle (usually 45°/45°, 30°/60°, or 60°/30°) and drawing the horizontal and vertical elements of the elevations to scale. They are sometimes called paraline drawings. An *isometric* drawing is a type of axonometric drawing that projects the view along x-, y-, and z-axes that are 120° apart.

Oblique drawings can be drawn relative to either the plan or the elevation. A plan oblique is another term for an axonometric drawing. An elevation oblique is projected from an elevation; the elevation closest to the viewer is shown to scale and actual shape, but the other sides of the building are foreshortened.

The answer is C.

22. A project architect assigns a project to two interns in the office who collaborate to complete the construction drawings and details for the design the project architect has sketched. The project architect answers occasional questions during the development of the drawings but does not review the drawings until they are 95% complete. Which type of quality management technique best describes the project architect's approach?

    A. total quality management

    B. quality control

    C. quality assurance

    D. coordination

Solution

Quality control requires a project architect or designated quality control reviewer to check the work immediately before it is distributed to the user. It helps to catch any errors that may have been made, but has the disadvantage of detecting them at the very end of the process, when they may be more costly to fix or when time may not allow for comprehensive revision of the drawings affected.

To help offset the disadvantages of quality control, quality assurance was developed. *Quality assurance* requires periodic checks of the work while it is being developed. For example, periodic "check sets" may be generated for the reviewer when the project is 25%, 50%, and 90% complete. This allows the reviewer to pick up errors earlier in the process and is intended to produce a better-coordinated set of documents.

Total quality management (TQM) goes beyond quality control and quality assurance, with the goal of customer satisfaction.

The answer is B.

PROJECT MANUAL AND SPECIFICATIONS

23. When incorporating the mechanical engineer's specifications into the project manual, the architect should establish all of the following EXCEPT the

    A. exact numbering system of the specification sections

    B. type of header and footer used on each page

    C. content of each specification section

    D. page layout of the specification sections

Solution

The architect is responsible for developing the overall format and appearance of the project manual and the specification sections. Each consultant is responsible for the content of their respective specifications.

The answer is C.

24. A specification section written following the recommendations of the Construction Specifications Institute would include all of the following sections EXCEPT

    A. administration

    B. execution

    C. general

    D. products

Solution

The three-part specification format developed by the Construction Specifications Institute (CSI) and Construction Specifications Canada (CSC) includes sections entitled *General*, *Products*, and *Execution*. The General section includes administrative and procedural requirements specific to the specification. The Products section includes information about materials, systems, manufactured units, shop fabrication, and factory finishing prior to installation. The Execution section gives instructions for on-site incorporation of the products into the project. A detailed description of the various articles and paragraphs included in each part is given in CSI's *SectionFormat*™.

> *Study Note:* Be familiar with the MasterFormat™ method of organizing specifications and other construction information, as well as with standard procedures for writing individual sections of the specifications and other parts of a project manual. A complete project manual typically contains the following: bidding requirements (including the invitation to bid, instructions to bidders, and bid forms), contract forms (including the agreement between owner and contractor, bonds, and certificates of insurance), general and supplementary conditions, and the technical specifications themselves.

The answer is A.

25. In the following specification, which item is described with a performance specification?

Part 2—Products

2.01 Metal Support Material

General: To the extent not otherwise indicated, comply with ASTM C754 for metal system supporting gypsum wallboard.

Ceiling suspension main runners: $1\frac{1}{2}$ in steel channels, cold rolled.

Hanger wire: ASTM A641, soft, Class 1 galvanized, prestretched; sized in accordance with ASTM C754.

Hanger anchorage devices: size for 3× calculated loads, except size direct-pull concrete inserts for 5× calculated loads.

Studs: ASTM C645; 25 gage, $2\frac{1}{2}$ in deep, except as otherwise indicated.

ASTM C645; 25 gage, $3\frac{5}{8}$ in deep.

ASTM C645; 20 gage, 6 in deep.

Runners: Match studs; type recommended by stud manufacturer for floor and ceiling support of studs, and for vertical abutment of drywall work at other work.

Furring members: ASTM C65; 25 gage, hat-shaped.

Fasteners: Type and size recommended by furring manufacturer for the substrate and application indicated.

A. fasteners
B. hanger wire
C. hanger anchorage devices
D. ceiling suspension main runners

Solution

The specification simply states how the hanger anchorage devices must perform; that is, they must support a certain amount of weight. As long as they do this, they can be any type, size, or style that the contractor selects. The requirements for the fasteners are those selected as appropriate by the manufacturer. The hanger wire specification is a reference type specification because it refers to a particular industry-standard specification. The ceiling suspension main runner is specified with a descriptive specification, which describes various qualities (size, material, and method of fabrication) of the ceiling runner.

The answer is C.

26. A reference to 3000 psi (20.7 MPa) concrete alludes to the concrete's

A. ultimate strength in psi (MPa)
B. strength in tension
C. flexural strength without reinforcing
D. design strength in psi (MPa) after curing for 28 days

Solution

The design strength of the final mix of concrete is specified by the compressive strength of the concrete in pounds per square inch (megapascals) after it has cured for 28 days, indicated with the variable f'_c. Common strengths are 3000 psi (20.7 MPa) and 4000 psi (27.6 MPa), although high-strength concrete is available up to 22,000 psi (150 MPa).

The answer is D.

27. Which of the following would not be found in a project manual?

A. bid log
B. subsurface soil conditions report, noted "for information only"
C. sitework specification
D. bid bond form

Solution

A bid log is used by the architect to record the bids as they are opened and to help the owner evaluate them. It is never included in the project manual.

A subsurface soil conditions report would not be a part of the contract documents, but may be included in the project manual and be designated "for information only." A sitework specification is one of the technical sections and would be included in the manual. The bid bond form would be included in the manual, but this is considered to be a bidding document, not part of the contract documents.

The answer is A.

28. A performance specification

A. allows innovation by the contractor
B. requires more work by the architect
C. is not appropriate for normal building products
D. all of the above

Solution

All of the responses are correct. A *performance specification* lets the contractor, material supplier, and fabricator decide how best to supply the required building component. Although performance specifications are detailed, there are many ways to satisfy them. They are more difficult to research, write, and review, so there is more work for the architect. For ordinary materials, there is usually no need to write performance specifications because the requirements are so well established in the construction industry.

The answer is D.

29.   Which of the following are likely to occur if the drawings and specifications are not thoroughly coordinated? (Choose the four that apply.)

   A.   a decrease of the actual cost from the estimated cost because the contractor bid on a less expensive material shown on the drawings, although the same material was called out as a more expensive type in the specifications
   B.   a lawsuit
   C.   the need for a change order during construction, to account for modifications required to correct discrepancies in the two documents
   D.   a delay in construction
   E.   an increase in cost because the contractor bid the least expensive choice between two conflicting requirements when the client wanted the more expensive option
   F.   the architect may be held financially responsible for the omission

Solution

It is commonly believed that the specifications take precedence over the drawings, but AIA Document A201 states that these two documents are considered "complementary and what is required by one shall be binding as if required by all." In cases where there is a discrepancy, the conflict should be brought to the architect's attention. Any time there are conflicts in the project documents, the best that can happen is a quick resolution with no change to the cost, but usually an increase results and the project may be delayed as the parties deal with administrative work. Conflicts in the documents can be corrected with an addendum prior to bidding or negotiation, by change order, or by modification after the construction contract is signed.

Litigation would be a last resort and other remedies would be sought and implemented before a lawsuit occurred.

The answer is C, D, E, and F.

30.   Which of the following types of specifications would probably NOT be used to specify asphalt roofing shingles?

   A.   descriptive
   B.   base bid with "approved equal" language
   C.   reference standard
   D.   base bid with alternates

Solution

A *base bid with alternates* type of specification for asphalt shingles is not appropriate because this type of specification would leave too much to the discretion of the contractor without provision for review by the architect. There are many different types of shingles available and this type of specification may leave the owner open to use of an inferior product.

A better specification would be the *base bid with "approved equal"* language. This would give the owner and architect more control over the types of products used during construction, because pre-approved manufacturers would be defined in the specification.

The answer is D.

31.   Which of the following statements about specifications are true? (Choose the two that apply.)

   A.   Both narrowscope and broadscope sections can be used in the same project manual.
   B.   Drawings are more binding than specifications if there is a conflict.
   C.   Specifications show quality; drawings show quantity.
   D.   Proprietary specifications encourage competitive bids.
   E.   Specifications should not be open to interpretation if they are the "base bid with alternates" type.
   F.   Proprietary specifications are the most difficult for an architect to write.

Solution

It is possible to use both narrowscope and broadscope specifications in the same project manual. It may be necessary to provide a more in-depth specification for an innovative construction technique, for example, than for concrete block or some other common construction material. Specifications are used to define the quality of products to be used in the project, while the drawings define the quantities of materials and where they are to be used.

AIA Document A201 states that the drawings and specifications are to be considered equally binding. *Proprietary specifications* do not encourage competitive bids because they refer to a specific product and do not allow substitutions. They are the easiest for an architect to write because they simply call out a product by name. A *base bid with alternates* allows a contractor to substitute products he or she deems equal without requiring the architect's approval. Therefore, they could be considered open to interpretation.

The answer is A and C.

32. Requirements for library checkout equipment are found in which division of the MasterFormat™ specifications?

   A. 10 10 00
   B. 11 05 00
   C. 12 45 00
   D. 13 80 00

Solution

Division 11, Equipment, is the CSI specification division for larger, specialty items. Division 10 is for smaller Specialties, Division 12 is for Furnishings, and Division 13 is for Special Construction.

The answer is B.

33. Which MasterFormat™ division would include the specification requirements for metal studs for interior partition walls?

   A. 05
   B. 09
   C. 10
   D. 13

Solution

Light-gage metal framing for interior partitions is specified in Division 09, Finishes.

The answer is B.

34. The procedure for submitting shop drawings for architectural woodwork is specified in MasterFormat™ Division

   A. 01
   B. 06
   C. 09
   D. 12

Solution

Procedures for submittals are found in Division 01, General Requirements. The requirements in individual technical sections refer to Division 01 to define procedural requirements and each section includes a list of the specific types of samples required for that product.

The answer is A.

35. Where would the requirements for testing a plumbing system be located?

   A. in a section of Division 1 of the specifications
   B. in Part 1 of Section 22 40 00, Plumbing
   C. in Part 2 of Section 22 40 00, Plumbing
   D. in Part 3 of Section 22 40 00, Plumbing

Solution

Requirements for testing of materials and equipment are in Part 3 of each technical section if appropriate to the specification.

The answer is D.

36. The specifications for a project state that all custom-built casework must comply with the AWI Quality Standards. Of which type of specification is this is an example?

   A. proprietary
   B. prescriptive
   C. descriptive
   D. reference

Solution

A *reference specification* requires a material or product to comply with the requirements of an independent testing laboratory or authority. Reference specifications are short and easy to write but require knowledge of which standards best apply to the situation at hand.

The answer is D.

CONTRACTUAL DOCUMENTS

37.   During the final stages of contract document development, the electrical engineer discovers that mechanical ductwork is shown on the mechanical engineering drawings in a position that interferes with electrical conduit. The person responsible for resolving this conflict is the

    A.   electrical engineer
    B.   mechanical engineer
    C.   contractor
    D.   architect

Solution

The architect is responsible for the overall coordination of all consultants' drawings and for resolving disputes and conflicts. The electrical engineer should bring the conflict to the architect's attention. The architect can then coordinate with both consultants to resolve the conflict.

The answer is D.

38.   A client requests that the architect provide a full-time staff member on the job site during construction. The architect is entitled to extra compensation for the service under what provision of AIA Document B141?

    A.   designated services
    B.   schedule of services
    C.   schedule of values
    D.   optional additional services

Solution

AIA Document B141 clearly states what constitutes evaluations of the work included in the standard scope of services: periodic site visits, but not exhaustive or continuous on-site inspections. On-site project representation is considered an additional service and is defined in the schedule of services.

The answer is B.

39.   AIA Document B141 separates the architect from the contractor with

    A.   agency
    B.   privity
    C.   mediation
    D.   indemnification

Solution

AIA Document B141 states that nothing in that agreement will create a contractual relationship with a third party against either the architect or the owner. This reinforces the idea of *privity*—two parties to a contract are not liable to a third party.

The answer is B.

40.   Which of the following may be used to encourage the contractor to finish the job or to satisfy mechanic's lien claims by subcontractors?

    A.   surety bond
    B.   liquidated damages
    C.   retainage
    D.   arbitration

Solution

Retainage, or an amount of money withheld from each pay application, gives the owner leverage to make the contractor finish the job and provides a reserve in case liens must be satisfied.

A *surety bond* involves a third party (the surety) who ensures completion of the project if the contractor fails to meet his or her obligations. *Liquidated damages* are an amount specified in advance that the contractor must pay to the owner if the project is not completed on time. *Arbitration* is a method of resolving disputes between parties to a contract.

The answer is C.

41.   Which of the following describes the architect's role as the owner's agent, as defined in AIA Document B141?

    A.   The architect acts on behalf of the owner, making decisions, expediting the work, and taking on responsibilities the owner would normally have.
    B.   The architect mediates between the owner, the contractor, and vendors for the benefit of the owner.
    C.   The architect is the principal of the relationship and balances the needs of the contractor and the owner.
    D.   The architect works for the owner in certain designated areas where he or she has been given the authority to act on the owner's behalf.

Solution

An *agent* acts on behalf of another and assumes certain specified authority and duties, but does not take on responsibilities another person normally would have.

The answer is D.

42.　Which of the following are parts of the contract documents?

I.　an addendum
II.　a change order
III.　special supplementary conditions
IV.　the contractor's bid
V.　a written amendment signed by owner and contractor

   A.　I, II, and IV only
   B.　I, III, and V only
   C.　I, II, III, and V only
   D.　II, III, IV, and V only

Solution

The contractor's bid, like other bidding documents, is not part of the contract documents unless specifically stated in the agreement.

The answer is C.

43.　Which of the following is the contractor solely responsible for?

I.　field reports to the owner
II.　field tests
III.　scaffolding
IV.　reviewing claims of subcontractors
V.　reviewing shop drawings

   A.　II and III only
   B.　IV and V only
   C.　I, II, and III only
   D.　II, III, and IV only

Solution

Scaffolding is part of the means of construction, which is the contractor's responsibility. The standard general conditions specifically state that the contractor is responsible for arranging and coordinating field tests.

Field reports are the responsibility of the architect, who is also responsible for reviewing claims. A subcontractor may make a claim directly to the contractor, who in turn would have to make a claim to the owner. Both the contractor and the architect are responsible for reviewing shop drawings, although only the contractor is responsible for the accuracy of the shop drawings. The architect reviews them only for general compliance with the requirements of the contract documents.

The answer is A.

44.　In a typical relationship established by AIA Document B141 (RAIC Document 6), who acts as the agent?

   A.　the architect
   B.　the contractor
   C.　the owner's attorney
   D.　the owner

Solution

In the relationship established by the standard owner-architect agreement, the architect is the agent, the owner is the principal, and the contractor is the third party. A legal advisor is not the agent in the relationship established by this agreement, but an attorney may act as the owner's agent in regard to legal matters.

The answer is A.

45.　What does the phrase "time is of the essence" mean in a contract?

   A.　The project must be completed as quickly as possible.
   B.　All work must be completed by the dates specified in the contract or the contractor has breached the agreement.
   C.　The contractor must mobilize its forces and begin working on the project as soon as the contract is signed.
   D.　The owner is responsible for setting the construction schedule.

Solution

When the dates included in the contract are firm, the contract will include the phrase "time is of the essence." By agreeing to the contract, the contractor is affirming that the construction period stated is a reasonable amount of time for completing the job and that the work will be completed by the specified date. If both parties (the contractor and the owner) do not fulfill their obligations by the dates stated in the contract, they may be in breach of the contract. This phrase is included in Subparagraph 8.2.1 of AIA Document

A201. If the contractual deadlines are not met, the contractor may be forced to pay the owner liquidated damages if this provision has been agreed upon in advance.

The answer is B.

46.   Which party owns the copyright on a building?

    A.   the owner
    B.   the architect
    C.   the contractor
    D.   the construction manager

Solution

The architect owns the copyright on his or her work from the moment the ideas are expressed in a tangible form, such as sketches, CAD files, technical drawings, models, and so on. These expressions that move a building from an idea to a built structure are known as *instruments of service* and are addressed in AIA Document B141, Subparagraph 1.3.2. Subparagraph 1.3.2.1 states that the architect retains ownership of the copyright. AIA Document A201, Subparagraph 1.6.1, informs the contractor of the architect's right to ownership and explains that although the contractor is permitted to use the instruments of service for the purposes of constructing that project, he may not use them for any other purpose.

The right to ownership of the instruments of service is of critical importance to architects, and all owner-architect agreements should contain language protecting this right. Architects bear responsibility for the way that these documents are used. AIA Document B141, Subparagraph 1.3.2.2, allows the owner a nonexclusive license to reproduce drawings for use on this project only. The owner does not own the design or the instruments of service, just the building that is constructed using them. If the owner wishes to build another building using the same design, the architect's consent must be obtained. This protects the architect from circumstances where drawings are being used without the architect's knowledge and without proper payment for architectural services. It also guards against situations where the drawings prepared specifically for one project are being used under conditions not addressed by the original documents, which may expose the architect to liability.

The answer is B.

BIDDING PROCEDURES AND DOCUMENTS

47.   Which of the following is NOT included in an advertisement to bid?

    A.   bid form
    B.   details on the size and scope of the project
    C.   details on the type and amount of bid security required
    D.   name of the owner

Solution

Bid forms are placed with the Instructions to Bidders in the project manual.

An advertisement to bid would be placed in a local newspaper or posted with a *plan room*, which is a place (physical or virtual/on-line) where contractors can obtain information about projects currently out for bid.

Among other information, the advertisement to bid typically includes the name and location of the project; name and address of the owner and architect; description and scope of the project, including major materials and construction systems; date, time, and location the bids are due; procedures for submitting bids; and type and amount of bid security required.

> *Study Note:* Understand the entire bidding process (construction procurement), including advertisement to bid, invitation to bid, availability of bid documents, substitutions, addenda, prebid conferences, bid opening procedures, and the evaluation and awarding of bids.

The answer is A.

48.   Addenda are issued

    A.   prior to bidding
    B.   after bidding and before the award of the contract
    C.   after the award of the contract
    D.   during construction

Solution

An *addendum* is a written or graphic document issued by the architect prior to bidding that modifies or interprets the bidding documents. Addenda may be issued in response to errors discovered in the bidding documents, changes the client wants to make, questions from bidders, or additions or deletions needed. Addenda must be sent to all bidders at least four days prior to the bid date.

The answer is A.

49.   A contractor bidding on a project submits a bid fifteen minutes late, after bid opening has started. According to AIA Document A701, *Instructions to Bidders* (CCDC Document 23, *A Guide to Calling Bids and Awarding Construction Contracts*), the architect should

- A.   allow the bid if there are no objections from the other bidders
- B.   return the sealed bid to the bidder, unopened
- C.   accept the bid, but review it later, after the other bids have been opened
- D.   stop the bidding procedure, and require that all bids be resubmitted at a later time

Solution

Paragraph 4.3.2 of AIA Document A701 (CCDC Document 23) requires that bids be deposited at the designated location prior to the time and date for receipt, and that bids submitted after that deadline be returned to the bidder unopened.

The answer is B.

50.   According to AIA Document A701, *Instructions to Bidders* (CCDC Document 23), bids must be submitted on

- A.   standard AIA (CCDC) bid forms
- B.   the contractor's standard bid form
- C.   forms provided with the bidding documents
- D.   forms provided by the owner

Solution

Paragraph 4.1.1 in AIA Document A701 (CCDC Document 23) states that bids shall be submitted on the forms included with the bidding documents. These forms are used because they can be tailored to meet the requirements for the project by including a listing of alternates and unit prices.

The answer is C.

51.   During bidding, a contractor wants to propose a substitution of a material specified in the contract documents. According to AIA Document A701, *Instructions to Bidders*, (CCDC Document 23), the request for substitution must be received by the architect ___ days prior to the receipt of bids. (Fill in the blank.)

Solution

According to AIA Document A701, *Instructions to Bidders* (CCDC Document 23), no substitutions can be considered unless a written request for such approval has been received by the architect at least ten days prior to the date for receipt of bids.

If the substitutions are approved, the architect must issue an addendum for the substitution approval no later than four days prior to the date for receipt of bids.

The answer is 10 days.

52.   The architect's drawings released for bidding indicate an area of exterior concrete paving with an indeterminate limit because the owner has not made a final decision concerning the amount of paved area wanted. In order to fairly compare bid prices for the paving, the architect may request on the bid form that the contractors include

- A.   individual quotes
- B.   unit prices
- C.   fixed costs
- D.   contingencies

Solution

A *unit price* is a set price quote, established by a contractor during bidding, for a specified amount of the work. The unit price is based on cost per unit of measurement, such as square foot (square meter), or linear foot (linear meter), or on individual units, such as a light fixture. Unit prices are requested on bid forms when the full extent of the work is unknown.

The answer is B.

53.   Which of the following would be used to formally incorporate a substitution into the work prior to award of the contract?

- A.   change order
- B.   addendum
- C.   alternate listing
- D.   construction change directive

Solution

Addenda are used to make changes to the contract documents after they are issued for bidding but before the contract is awarded. *Change orders* and *construction change directives* also modify the original contract documents, but they are used after the contract is awarded. An *alternate listing* is simply the list of alternates that the contractor must include in the bid.

The answer is B.

54.   Which of the following may be part of the bidding documents?

I.   specifications
II.   invitation to bid
III. list of subcontractors
IV.   owner-contractor agreement
V.   performance bond

    A.   I, III, and IV only
    B.   II, III, and IV only
    C.   I, II, IV, and V only
    D.   I, II, III, IV, and V

Solution

All of the items listed can be a part of the bidding documents, although all of these documents are not always included. Of the five, a list of subcontractors is used least frequently.

The answer is D.

55.   At the scheduled time for a bid opening, a contractor comes rushing into the room three minutes late, clutching his bid. None of the bids has been opened yet. What should the architect do?

    A.   Refuse to accept the bid, stating that the deadline has passed.
    B.   Since none of the bids have been opened yet, ask the other bidders if they would object to accepting the late bid.
    C.   Accept the bid with prejudice.
    D.   Accept the bid because none have been opened, but make a mental note to look on it with disfavor while you are evaluating it.

Solution

The contractor was only three minutes late, and—more important—none of the bids has been opened. In light of these facts, the most reasonable approach would be to ask the other bidders if there is an objection. If not, accept the bid.

However, if any of the bids had been opened, it would certainly not be advisable to accept late submittals, nor should a bid that is three minutes late be prejudiced if it is accepted, simply because it was late.

The answer is B.

56.   Which of the following statements about bidding is generally FALSE?

    A.   Bidding procedures must be clearly and extensively outlined in the instructions to bidders because there are so many variations of the procedures.
    B.   Bidding is nearly always required for federally funded projects.
    C.   Open bidding usually presents more problems than other types.
    D.   Competitive bidding takes more time than negotiation but can result in a lower construction cost.

Solution

Bidding procedures should always be clearly stated, but not because there are so many variables. In fact, bidding procedures are fairly well established in the construction industry, regardless of whether there is open bidding or private bid openings.

Government-funded projects at the federal, state, or local level are generally required to bid.

Open bidding means that nearly anyone can bid, regardless of experience. This encourages a variety of contractors to participate, but when bidding is open, it can be difficult to evaluate qualified bidders. In addition, the cost and complexity of advertising and administering the bidding process may increase.

The bid process can lengthen total project time due to the time alloted for review of the construction documents and contract negotiation, but the competitive nature of bidding allows the owner to compare prices before hiring a contractor.

The answer is A.

57.   A performance bond

    A.   ensures that subcontractors complete their work
    B.   guarantees that the contractor will finish on time
    C.   covers any possible liens that may be filed on the building
    D.   protects the owner by having a third party responsible for completing the work if the contractor does not

Solution

A *performance bond* is issued by a surety company that obligates itself to finish a project should the contractor default.

A *labor and material payment bond* is designed to pay liens if they occur. Other provisions of the owner-contractor agreement, such as liquidated damages, are designed to encourage the contractor to finish on time. The general contractor is responsible for the performance of the subcontractors under provisions of AIA Document A201 (CCDC Document 2).

The answer is D.

58.   If the lowest bid comes in 20% over a client's construction budget, the architect should advise the client to

    A.   increase the budget
    B.   rebid the project using another list of contractors
    C.   collaborate on revising the scope of the project to reduce cost
    D.   accept all the deduct alternates, to reduce the bid, and authorize a slight increase in construction cost to bring the two closer together

Solution

The most reasonable alternative is for the owner and architect to work together to make adjustments to the design to comply with the budget. The architect is obligated to make these revisions under the provisions of AIA Document B141 (RAIC Document 6).

It is unlikely that the client could afford to increase the budget, or would consider that an acceptable alternative. Rebidding the project, even with a different group of contractors, would probably not result in much, if any, cost savings. Accepting all the deduct alternates might not be a desirable course of action and may not even be enough to compensate for the cost overrun. It is better to consider the project holistically and make changes to bring it in within the budget.

The answer is C.

59.   What variable affects a bid the most?

    A.   the contractor's profit margin
    B.   the influences of the construction marketplace
    C.   labor and materials
    D.   subcontract bids

Solution

Labor and materials, by far, have the biggest influence on the cost of a job because they represent about 80% of the cost. Labor and materials costs influence the amount of subcontractors' bids. Profit tends to be based on a percentage of the construction cost, and market influences do not have as great an effect on overall costs as the raw costs of the labor and materials required to construct the project.

The answer is C.

60.   Procedures a bidder must follow to propose a substitution will be found in the

    A.   advertisement to bid
    B.   bidding procedures
    C.   instructions to bidders
    D.   general conditions

Solution

During bidding, the procedure a contractor must follow to propose a substitution is defined in the instructions to bidders. After the contract is awarded, if the contractor wishes to propose a substitution, he or she must consult the instructions in the general requirements of the specifications. The advertisement to bid simply states that bidding is being accepted for a particular project and gives information about how to submit a bid. There is no such document as "bidding procedures."

The answer is C.

61.   When the owner wants to make sure some amount of money is included in the bid before the exact specification for the item is known, the architect should use

    A.   an allowance
    B.   an add alternate
    C.   a material bond
    D.   a unit price

Solution

When the owner wants to make sure some amount of money is included in the bid before the exact amount of the item is known, the architect should use an *allowance*. For example, the contractor may be asked to include a $10,000 allowance on a residential project for kitchen appliances. This gives the architect and owner the opportunity to choose the appliances at a later date. If the cost of the selected appliances exceeds the allowance, the contractor is owed the difference.

Alternates are used to require the contractor to provide an alternate price for something that varies from the base bid. Alternates can be either "add" or "deduct" depending on the change to the contract amount. A *material bond* is a way to guarantee payment for materials by a bonding company. A *unit price* is a way to obtain a price commitment from a contractor on a portion of work before the total quantity of the work is known.

The answer is A.

62.   The final responsibility for awarding a construction contract rests with the

    A.   architect
    B.   construction manager
    C.   owner
    D.   owner's legal counsel

Solution

The owner is ultimately responsible for deciding which contractor will be hired for a project. The architect is generally involved in the decision making process, but only assists and gives advice to the owner.

The answer is C.

63.   Which of the following is the most appropriate way to announce bid results?

    A.   The architect should make a statement at the conclusion of the bid opening identifying the apparent low bidder.
    B.   After evaluating all of the bids, the owner should make a decision of award and the architect should notify the bidders.
    C.   The architect should call all of the bidders and give them the results.
    D.   The owner should publish the bid results in the local newspaper.

Solution

During a bid opening, the architect or a designated representative will open the bids, read them aloud, and record in a bid log the base bid amounts, bids for proposed alternates, receipt of addenda, and whether required supporting documentation is included with the bid (such as a bid bond). The architect should not announce the apparent low bidder at the bid opening.

The owner should evaluate the bids and make a decision about the award within a reasonable amount of time. The

architect may then notify all of the bidders of the owner's decision. The delay allows time for the owner to complete evaluation of the bids and also provides an opportunity for a contractor to retract a bid in the event that a mathematical error is discovered after submission.

The answer is B.

CONSTRUCTION ADMINISTRATION SERVICES

64.   According to AIA Document A201, *General Conditions of the Contract for Construction* (CCAC Document 2, *Stipulated Price Contract*), which of the following methods CANNOT be used to make changes in the work once construction has started?

    A.   work modification form
    B.   order for minor change in the work
    C.   change order
    D.   construction change directive

Solution

A *work modification form* is not an acceptable way to change the scope of the work. According to Article 7 of AIA Document A201, changes in the work can be made by *change order*, *construction change directive*, or *order for a minor change in the work* without invalidating the contract, subject to limitations in the article and elsewhere in the contract documents.

> *Study Note:* Be thoroughly familiar with AIA (CCAC/ CCDC) document provisions concerning change orders and the procedures used in making changes in the work.

The answer is A.

65.   When a contractor proposes a substitution of a material or method of construction that is specified in the contract documents, the architect's responsibility in reviewing the substitution includes

    A.   proving that the proposed substitution is equivalent to the original
    B.   finding documentation that relates to the substitution
    C.   forwarding the request to the owner
    D.   approving or disapproving the request

Solution

Any request for substitution by the contractor must be made in writing and must be accompanied by a complete description of the proposed substitution, including drawings, test data, and other information necessary for an evaluation. The burden of proof of the merit of the substitution falls upon the contractor. The architect only has to review the submission and either approve or disapprove it.

The answer is D.

66.   During a site visit, the architect notes that the contractor is using unapproved materials that were not originally specified. Before work can be stopped under the provisions of AIA Document A201 (CCAC Document 2), what must occur?

    A.   The contractor must show cause why the unapproved materials are being used.

    B.   The owner must issue a written order to the contractor to stop the work.

    C.   The architect must give written notice of intent to stop the work and wait seven days.

    D.   The architect, with the approval of the owner, must issue a stop work order.

Solution

Only the owner has the right to stop the work, according to the provisions of Article 2 of AIA Document A201 (CCAC Document 2). The owner may stop the work if the contractor fails to correct work not in accordance with the requirements of the contract documents or persistently fails to carry out work in accordance with the contract documents.

Article 3.4 (CCAC Document 2) states that the contractor may make substitutions only with the consent of the owner, after evaluation by the architect and with a change order.

    Study Note: Review the provisions of the standard general conditions that relate to the owner's responsibilities, including the information provided by the owner and the owner's right to carry out the work.

The answer is B.

67.   During construction, the architect suspects that an incorrect type of plumbing piping has been installed. However, the contractor has covered the work with a partition because the architect did not request in advance to examine it. The architect now requests that the contractor tear out a portion of the partition in order to facilitate inspection. Upon review, the plumbing is found to be incorrect. The party responsible for the cost of uncovering the work is the

    A.   architect

    B.   owner

    C.   contractor

    D.   plumbing subcontractor

Solution

Article 12 of AIA Document A201 (CCAC Document 2), states that if no specific request has been made to examine work, and if the work is subsequently covered, the owner must pay for the uncovering if the work is found to conform to the contract documents. If the work is found not to conform to the contract documents, then the contractor is responsible for the cost of uncovering the work.

The answer is C.

68.   During construction, the architect is obligated to visit the site to keep the client informed about the progress and quality of the work. According to the basic provisions of AIA Document B141 (RAIC Document 6) these visits must occur

    A.   every week

    B.   every two weeks

    C.   as appropriate to the stage of the contractor's operations

    D.   only if they have been written into the agreement as extra services

Solution

Site visits are part of the basic services of contract administration, but no specific time interval for them is given in the contract. AIA Document B141 states that the architect shall visit the site at intervals appropriate to the stage of the contractor's operations or as agreed by the owner and architect. RAIC Document 6 requires that the architect keep the client informed of the progress and quality of work observed during the course of the general review/field review, but also does not give any specific time intervals.

The answer is C.

69. During a site visit, the architect notices that a worker has installed studs using a spacing that is not in accordance with the drawings. Under the provisions of AIA Document A201 (CCAC Document 2) the authority to reject this work rests with the

    A. architect
    B. owner
    C. owner and architect
    D. general contractor

Solution

According to AIA Document A201 (CCAC Document 2), the architect has the authority to reject work that does not conform to the contract documents.

The answer is A.

70. During construction, the contractor makes a claim to the architect to extend the contract time because the property owner delayed in supplying certain equipment. Under AIA Document A201 (CCAC Document 2) which of the following actions by the architect is NOT permitted?

    A. Tell the owner and contractor that a determination cannot be made, due to a lack of information.
    B. Request additional information from the contractor.
    C. Refer the claim to the owner's attorney.
    D. Suggest a compromise.

Solution

Under the provisions of Article 4.4.2 of AIA Document A201 (CCAC Document 2), when reviewing a claim, the architect must take one or more of the following actions: 1) approve the claim, 2) reject the claim, 3) suggest a compromise, 4) request additional supporting data from the claimant or a response with supporting data from the other party, or 5) advise the parties that the architect is unable to resolve the claim due to a lack of sufficient information to evaluate the merits of the claim or because the architect concludes that it would be inappropriate for the architect to resolve the claim.

The answer is C.

71. Before finish work has started, the architect reminds the contractor that moisture tests are required by the specifications for all concrete on which resilient flooring will be placed. The party responsible for the cost of the tests is the

    A. architect
    B. owner
    C. contractor
    D. flooring subcontractor

Solution

Article 13.5 of AIA Document A201 (CCAC Document 2) states that tests, inspections, and approvals of portions of the work required by the contract documents or by laws, ordinances, rules, regulations, or orders of public authorities shall be paid for by the contractor. The contractor must also make arrangements for the tests and notify the architect of when they will be conducted.

Study Note: If testing becomes required *after* receipt of bids or after contract negotiations and is *not* part of the original contract documents, then the owner becomes responsible for paying for the testing. This provision applies to testing required by the architect, owner, or public authorities having jurisdiction. This situation might happen if the building field inspector requires a test that was not anticipated.

The answer is C.

72. A pressure test on plumbing supply piping required by the specifications reveals a leak in the system. According to AIA Document A201 (CCAC Document 2) the responsibility for fixing the leak and paying for a follow-up test rests with the

    A. owner
    B. contractor
    C. plumbing subcontractor
    D. owner and contractor jointly

Solution

Although the plumbing subcontractor may ultimately reimburse the contractor, according to AIA Document A201 (CCAC Document 2), the contractor is responsible for all costs made necessary by failures, including costs of repeated tests.

The answer is B.

73.   A change order can be requested by the

    A.   architect
    B.   owner
    C.   architect or owner
    D.   architect, owner, or contractor

Solution

Any of the three parties may request or suggest a change order. The paperwork is prepared by the architect, and all three parties must agree to and sign it.

Study Note: Understand the three ways changes can be made during construction: through change order, construction change directive, or minor change in the work.

The answer is D.

74.   According to AIA Document A201, the contractor may reasonably ask for an extension in the contract time without penalty for all of the following reasons EXCEPT

    A.   an owner's stop work order
    B.   slow work by a subcontractor
    C.   the architect's delay in approving shop drawings
    D.   labor disputes

Solution

Article 8.3 of AIA Document A201 states the reasons for an extension to the contract time. Slow work by a subcontractor does not constitute a valid reason. The contractor is responsible for keeping the project on schedule unless there are mitigating circumstances as stated in Article 8.3.

The answer is B.

75.   Which of the following parties are required to agree to a construction change directive?

    A.   architect and owner
    B.   architect and contractor
    C.   owner and contractor
    D.   architect, owner, and contractor

Solution

Article 7.1.2 of AIA Document A201 states that a construction change directive requires agreement by the owner and architect and *may or may not* be agreed to by the contractor.

The answer is A.

76.   During foundation construction, the property owner directs the architect to have the contractor reposition an upper-floor door by 3 ft (1 m). The wall has not yet been framed, and this relocation does not affect any other construction. The architect should notify the contractor of this change with

    A.   an addendum
    B.   a change order
    C.   a construction change directive
    D.   an order for a minor change in the work

Solution

This type of change would probably not require a change in the contracted sum or time and would not be inconsistent with the intent of the contract documents, so the architect may direct the change with an *order for a minor change in the work* (with or without the owner's approval).

Study Note: If this type of alteration is requested after the door opening is framed, it will probably involve a change in the contract sum and time, so a change order will be required. If the change is needed but the parties cannot immediately agree to the provisions of the adjustment (due to reasons of time, money, or both), a construction change directive can be used, and the time or money provisions are worked out at a later time.

The answer is D.

77.   During construction, the contractor asks the architect to approve a substitution for the floor tile originally specified, because the proposed new tile can be delivered faster. According to AIA Document A201 (CCAC Document 2), which of the following statements are true about this request?

I.   the owner's consent is required
II.   if approved, the tile will not be covered by warranty
III. the substitution must be made with a change order
IV.   the architect must evaluate the request

    A.   I and II only
    B.   III and IV only
    C.   I, III, and IV only
    D.   II, III, and IV only

Solution

Article 3.4.2 in AIA Document A201 (CCAC Document 2) states that the contractor may make substitutions only with the owner's consent, after evaluation by the architect and in accordance with a change order. The substitution will be covered by warranty.

The answer is C.

78.   According to AIA Document A201 (CCAC Document 2) the architect's duties when processing the contractor's application for payment include all of the following EXCEPT

    A.   comparing work done and materials stored to the contractor's schedule of values

    B.   making an exhaustive on-site inspection to verify that work has been completed properly

    C.   approving a certificate for payment if the architect feels the contractor is due payment in the amount stated

    D.   using previous site visits to determine that the work is in accordance with the contract documents

Solution

Article 9.4.2 of AIA Document A201 (CCAC Document 2) specifically states that the issuance of a certificate for payment is *not* a representation that the architect has 1) made exhaustive or continuous on-site inspections, 2) reviewed construction means, methods, techniques, sequences, or procedures, 3) reviewed copies of requisitions received from subcontractors and other data, or 4) made examination to ascertain how or for what purpose the contractor has used money previously paid.

Study Note: Understand the entire process of payments and completion.

The answer is B.

79.   According to AIA (CCAC/CCDC) Documents, the amount of retainage withheld from each application for payment is

    A.   5% of the amount due

    B.   10% of the amount due

    C.   10% of the total contract price

    D.   as stated in the owner-contractor agreement

Solution

The amount of retainage is determined and defined in AIA Document A101 (CCDC Document 2). The exact percentage is whatever is agreed to by the parties involved. The percentage of retainage can differ for work done and for stored materials.

The answer is D.

80.   When reviewing applications for payment, which of the following does the architect do? (Choose the four that apply.)

    A.   verify that adequate safety precautions are being observed by the contractor

    B.   determine if the completed work will be in accordance with the contract documents

    C.   become generally familiar with the progress and quality of the work

    D.   keep the owner informed about the progress of the work

    E.   check if the quantities of the installed work are as required by the contract documents

    F.   endeavor to guard the owner against defects in the work

Solution

AIA Document B141 (RAIC Document 6) states the reasons the architect visits the site and his or her responsibilities regarding applications for payment. When reviewing pay applications, the architect is responsible for determining whether work completed complies with the requirements of the contract documents. He or she should be generally familiar with the progress of the work and communicate this to the owner. The goal of the architect's involvement and review should be to endeavor to guard the owner against defects in the work.

The architect is not responsible for safety at the site or for the means, methods, or techniques of construction, including verifying quantities of materials.

Study Note: Review all of the listed duties and responsibilities of the architect contained in both AIA Document B141 and AIA Document A201 (CCDC Document 2 and RAIC Document 6).

The answer is B, C, D, and F.

81.   During a construction phase site visit, the architect notices that a finish subcontractor is not installing a flooring material properly. What should be the architect's first response?

    A.   Inform the owner in writing of the situation.

    B.   Withhold the appropriate amount on the contractor's application for payment.

    C.   Tell the contractor the work is not in conformance with the contract documents.

    D.   Notify the subcontractor that their work is not being properly installed.

Solution

According to AIA Document A201 (CCAC Document 2), communication by and with subcontractors and materials suppliers shall be through the contractor. The architect should inform the contractor of the improper installation, and the contractor is responsible for coordinating the repair with the subcontractor.

The answer is C.

82.   During the punch list inspection, the architect notices several items that are not completed and that will make it impossible for the client to occupy the space. According to AIA Document A201 (CCAC Document 2), which of the following actions must the architect take?

  A.   Notify the owner of the incomplete items.
  B.   Notify the contractor that there are unfinished items that must be finished before the project will be determined substantially complete.
  C.   Prepare a certificate of substantial completion with a list of incomplete items attached.
  D.   Revise the punch list and resubmit it to the contractor.

Solution

Document A201 (CCAC Document 2) requires that the architect notify the contractor of the unfinished items if they are not sufficiently complete in accordance with the contract documents, so that the owner can occupy the work or a designated portion thereof for its intended use. This must happen before the architect can issue a certificate of substantial completion.

The answer is B.

83.   After reviewing an application for payment, the architect decides to withhold the certificate for payment under the provisions of AIA Document A201 (CCAC Document 2). Which of the following statements about this situation is true?

  A.   The architect needs to withhold the entire amount.
  B.   The architect must notify the owner, who then notifies the contractor.
  C.   The architect and contractor must agree on a revised amount.
  D.   The architect can nullify a previous certificate to protect the owner.

Solution

The architect can nullify a previous certificate to protect the owner.

AIA Document A201 (CCAC Document 2) allows the architect to withhold the whole amount or a partial amount. If payment is to be withheld, the architect must notify the owner and contractor. The architect and contractor do not necessarily have to agree on the amount, although they should attempt to arrive at a mutually agreeable sum that accurately represents the amount of work completed.

The answer is D.

84.   A project is substantially complete when

  A.   the work is finished except for items on the punch list
  B.   the architect has determined that the building is nearly finished
  C.   the contractor has notified the architect that the work is complete
  D.   the owner can utilize the building for its intended use

Solution

Substantial completion means that the work or a designated portion of the work is sufficiently complete in accordance with the contract documents so that the owner can occupy or utilize the work for its intended use. A building can be substantially complete while still having minor items that the contractor must finish.

The answer is D.

85.   According to AIA Document A201 (CCAC Document 2), the contractor must submit an affidavit that all bills have been paid by the contractor before the owner's final payment is made. This affidavit must be submitted to the

  A.   architect
  B.   owner
  C.   owner's surety
  D.   owner's attorney

Solution

Various documents required prior to final payment must be submitted to the architect. The architect then forwards them to the owner while keeping a copy for the project records.

The answer is A.

86. Upon completion of the work, which of the following items must the contractor submit? (Choose the four that apply.)

   A. extra stock of materials listed in the specifications
   B. a certificate of occupancy
   C. copies of all change orders completed during the course of the work
   D. warranties and operating instructions
   E. certificates of inspection
   F. certificates of testing

Solution

AIA Document A201 (CCAC Document 2) requires that attic stock, a certificate of occupancy, warranties and operating instructions, and inspection certificates be submitted at project closeout. Copies of change orders are not required at this time, as this paperwork would be issued throughout the course of the project. Certificates of testing are required to be submitted to the architect promptly after each test, not at the completion of the work.

   Study Note: In addition to the items listed in the question, the contractor must also submit to the architect all documents required with the application for final payment, maintenance contracts, and a set of record drawings if required by the contract documents.

The answer is A, B, D, and E.

87. Which of the following is probably of LEAST concern to a subcontractor?

   A. the number of times equipment must be mobilized
   B. the types of tools needed to build a project
   C. workers' skill level needed to complete the work
   D. other trades that will be working on the same part of the construction at the same time

Solution

A subcontractor would be most interested in the number of times equipment must be brought to a job site, what kinds of workers will be required to complete the work, and possible interference with other trades, because all of these have cost and time implications. The types of tools needed may, under some circumstances, have some bearing on cost if they must be purchased or rented, but normally tools are available and do not represent a significant portion of the total cost.

To a certain extent, the architect can control these variables and therefore exercise some control over cost by designing and detailing so that construction may proceed in the most straightforward manner.

The answer is B.

88. An architect is reviewing shop drawings for a decorative wood grille wallcovering in a building lobby. The grille is attached to a gypsum board partition with metal clips. In what probable order of importance should the following items be checked?

I.   the spacing and size of the screws holding the clips to the partition
II. the possibility of splintering due to the way the exposed surfaces are milled
III. the flame-spread rating
IV. the method of cleaning the grille based on design and finish techniques used
V.   the local code requirements for surface finishes

   A. I, II, III, V, then IV
   B. III, V, II, IV, then I
   C. III, I, V, IV, then II
   D. V, III, I, II, then IV

Solution

Of the four detailing considerations implied by the choices (structural integrity, safety from contact, fire safety, and maintainability), fire safety is the most important, which would include verifying the code requirements for surface finishes and the actual flame-spread rating of the specified material. Next, the architect should verify the attachment method and structural integrity of the grille. Subsequently, the reviewer should verify the finish of the material to ensure it will not splinter or break, which could cause injury. Finally, the architect may choose to examine the material's maintainability.

The answer is D.

89.   A project is about 60% complete when the owner begins receiving field reports from the architect stating that the contractor is failing to properly supervise the job, which is resulting in incorrect work. After receiving several unsatisfactory reports, the owner becomes concerned about the contractor's performance and progress and asks the architect for advice. What should be done if the work is being performed under the conditions of AIA Document A201?

A.   After receiving the architect's field reports, the owner should stop the work and arrange for a meeting between the owner, architect, and contractor to determine the cause of the problems and what the contractor intends to do. If the contractor does not correct the work, the owner may carry out the work with other contractors and deduct the cost of the repairs from the original contractor's construction cost by change order.

B.   The architect should recommend that the owner give the contractor written notice of nonconformance with the contract documents and if, after seven days, the contractor has not begun corrective measures, the owner should terminate the contract.

C.   The architect and owner should discuss the problem to see if the owner would be willing to accept the nonconforming work in exchange for a reduction in the contract sum. If not, the owner should give seven days' written notice to terminate the contract. The owner has the option of finding another contractor to finish the job.

D.   The architect should, with the owner's knowledge, reject nonconforming work and notify the contractor that it must be corrected promptly. The architect should then remind the owner that the owner can have the work corrected after giving the contractor one seven-day written notice to correct the work and then an additional three days with a written notice.

Solution

The first step is to officially notify the contractor that the work is incorrect. The architect must do this in writing. The incorrect work should be rejected, and the contractor should be told to promptly correct it in accordance with the contract. If the contractor does not correct the work, the owner should be aware of the alternative courses of action available, up to and including terminating the contract. However, it is a better course of action for the owner to correct the work with his or her own forces (if the contractor refuses) than to terminate the original construction contract.

Stopping the work always has a detrimental effect on the entire project, and it does not provide for the normal notice to the contractor of nonconforming work. Quick termination of the contract without trying other remedies is not in accordance with the contract.

The contractor should always be notified in writing of any problems with the work and asked to correct the situation. The owner does have the option of accepting nonconforming work, but this is often not the best course of action because it can lead to disagreement about what amount should be deducted from the contract sum for acceptance of the nonconforming work.

The answer is D.

90.   The owner may NOT

A.   stop work if the contractor's performance is not satisfactory or is at variance with the contract documents

B.   carry on the work and deduct costs normally due to the contractor for any corrections required because of unsatisfactory work

C.   stop the work if the architect reports safety problems on the site

D.   refuse to give the contractor proof that he or she can meet the financial obligations of the project

Solution

AIA Document A201 states that the owner is obligated to furnish the contractor with reasonable evidence that financial arrangements have been made to fulfill his or her obligations under the contract. This document authorizes the owner to stop work for deficiencies in performance or safety violations or carry on the work with the owner's own forces to correct portions of the project where the contractor's performance is unsatisfactory and deduct the costs of the corrections from the contract sum.

The answer is D.

91. In what order should the following project closeout activities take place?

I.   prepare the final certificate for payment
II. compile punch list
III. issue the certificate of substantial completion
IV. receive notification from the contractor that the project is ready for final inspection
V.   receive consent of surety to release final payment

    A. II, III, V, IV, then I
    B. II, IV, III, V, then I
    C. IV, II, V, I, then III
    D. IV, V, II, III, then I

Solution

The contractor must notify the architect when the project is ready for the punch list inspection. Notification for final inspection comes after the punch list. During this final inspection, the architect verifies that the project has been completed according to the contract documents and the contractor is entitled to final payment. The issuance of a certificate of substantial completion comes after the final inspection. If this is followed by the consent of surety, the final payment certificate can be prepared.

The answer is B.

92. Substantial completion indicates

    A. that the owner can make use of the work for its intended purpose, and the requirements of the contract documents have been fulfilled
    B. that the contractor has completed correction of all punch list items
    C. that the final certificate for payment has been issued by the architect, and all documentation has been delivered to the owner
    D. the date on which the contractor prepares the punch list

Solution

Substantial completion is the point at which the owner can make use of the work for its intended purpose, and the requirements of the contract documents have been fulfilled. This is a critical point in construction because it marks the date that the building owner assumes the warranty on equipment. It is possible for a project to be deemed substantially complete even if punch list items remain incomplete.

The answer is A.

93. During a periodic visit to the site, the architect notices what appears to be an undersized variable air volume box being installed. What should the architect do?

    A. Tell the mechanical engineer to look at the situation during the next site visit by the engineer. Note the observation on a field report.
    B. Find the contractor and stop work on the installation until the size of the unit can be verified by the mechanical engineer and compared to the contract documents.
    C. Notify the owner in writing that the work is not proceeding according to the contract documents and advise him to stop the work until the architect can arrange a meeting with the mechanical engineer to resolve the situation.
    D. Notify the contractor that the equipment may be undersized, and have the contractor check on it. Concurrently, ask the mechanical engineer to verify the size of the unit against the specifications and report to the architect.

Solution

The architect has a duty to cooperate with the contractor and should at least mention the potential problem during the site visit. The contractor then has the opportunity to check on the equipment while the architect is following up with the mechanical engineer. The observation should be noted on the architect's field report to keep the client informed of the progress of the work. If, in fact, the equipment being installed is incorrect, corrective action may be taken. When the contractor is notified immediately, he or she can decide whether or not to suspend work on the installation of the equipment until the situation is resolved.

By the time the mechanical engineer is notified and visits the site, the installation of the equipment may have proceeded to a point where it is difficult to remedy. It is best to act quickly to keep the project moving while the issue is resolved. The architect does not have the authority to stop the work. It is not necessary to advise the owner to stop work which would only delay the project and add expense at this point.

The answer is D.

94. When the project is 90% complete, the code inspector requires installation of six exit signs in addition to those shown on the approved plans. Which of the following instruments should the architect use?

    A. order for minor change
    B. addendum
    C. change order
    D. construction change directive

Solution

Because the additional exit signs would necessitate an increase in construction cost and possibly in contract time, an *order for minor change* would not be appropriate. An *addendum* can only be used before the contract is signed. It is possible that the contractor and owner might disagree with the cost of the additional exit signs and a *construction change directive* would be used initially, but it is more likely that everyone would realize the need for the extra signs and agree on a price. Ultimately, a *change order* would be issued to adjust the contract sum.

The answer is C.

95. Which of the following statements about submittals is FALSE?

    A. The architect must review them prior to checking by the contractor.
    B. The contractor is ultimately responsible for the accuracy of dimensions and quantities.
    C. Submittals are not considered part of the contract documents.
    D. The contractor can reject submittals and request resubmittal by his or her subcontractors.

Solution

The contractor must review submittals prior to giving them to the architect.

The answer is A.

96. A contractor makes a claim for additional money for extra work caused by unforeseen circumstances. According to AIA Document A201, the architect must respond within _____ days. (Fill in the blank.)

Solution

AIA Document A201 specifically states that the architect must respond within 10 days of notification of the claim by the contractor. An acceptable response is to ask for supporting data to further document the claim.

The answer is 10 days.

97. Which of the following is NOT considered a submittal?

    A. mock-ups
    B. product data
    C. samples
    D. shop drawings

Solution

Product data, *samples*, and *shop drawings* may all be provided by the contractor for the architect's review. This documentation is known as a *submittal*.

A *mock-up* is a full-sized sample of a portion of the construction, commonly built on the job site. It can be either separate from the building or, if approved, can be integrated into the building. A mock-up is called for in individual sections of the specifications for items that will be repeated throughout the project, innovative construction techniques, and other instances where it is useful to see the "finished product" before it is truly finished. Mock-ups can be very expensive, so they should only be specified where necessary. They become more cost effective if the approved mock-up can then be integrated into the building.

The answer is A.

98. The architect's submittal log entries should include all of the following EXCEPT the

    A. action taken
    B. contract name
    C. date of receipt of the submittal
    D. date of forwarding to the consultant

Solution

The contract name need not be included with each log entry because the submittal log itself will be identified with the project name and number.

The answer is B.

99. A construction change directive requires the signature(s) of the

    A. architect only
    B. architect and contractor only
    C. architect and owner only
    D. architect, owner, and contractor

Solution

A *construction change directive* requires the signatures of the architect and owner only. A minor change in the work only requires the architect's signature. A change order requires the signatures of all three parties. No document requires just the architect's and contractor's signatures.

The answer is C.

PROJECT AND PRACTICE MANAGEMENT

100. During negotiations to develop a final, fixed construction cost with a preselected contractor, the owner wants to reduce the cost of construction suggested by the architect's original cost estimate. The architect should advise the owner to

    A. suggest that the project be put out to bid if the price is too high
    B. set a fixed limit on the construction cost, and negotiate directly with the subcontractors
    C. establish contractual penalties for exceeding the architect's original estimate
    D. consider the contractor's recommendations for alternate construction methods

Solution

On a negotiated project, the contractor is in the best position to recommend alternate materials and construction methods that will lower costs while still meeting the owner's design requirements.

Bidding the project is no guarantee that the price will be lower; in fact, it may go up. The owner should not negotiate with subcontractors; that is the contractor's responsibility. Simply setting an arbitrary limit on construction cost does not encourage a lower price and is a punitive way to limit costs during negotiation.

The answer is D.

101. An architect has been hired to design an addition to a building of historical significance. Part of the project includes renovating and remodeling a portion of the existing building. The architect suggests that the owner retain the services of a historic preservation consultant. In order for the architect to make optimal use of the consultant's work, the owner should hire the consultant

    A. as soon as possible
    B. after schematic design work has been completed
    C. after the design development phase
    D. on an as-needed basis for technical questions

Solution

In general, consultants should be hired as soon as possible on a project so they can advise on initial scope and design direction as well as on more technical questions.

The answer is A.

102. For aesthetic reasons, the architect's specifications on a building project call for a specific method of constructing a concrete wall and slab that is not in accordance with normal construction practices. The contractor tells the architect that the contractor believes the specified method will create unsafe conditions. According to AIA Document A201 (CCAC Document 2), what action must the contractor take?

    A. Proceed with construction following the instructions in the specifications.
    B. Notify the architect in writing, and propose alternate methods of construction.
    C. Give written notice to both the owner and architect of the safety concerns, and wait for instruction from the architect.
    D. Modify the method to make it safe, and proceed with construction.

Solution

Generally, the contractor is solely responsible for the means and methods of construction, unless the contract documents give specific instructions to the contrary. However, upon determining that the instructions create an unsafe situation, the contractor must give timely written notice to the owner and architect and not proceed with the unsafe portion of the work until receipt of further written instructions from the architect. If the contractor is instructed to proceed regardless of the safety concerns raised, the owner becomes solely responsible for any resulting loss or damage.

    Study Note: Review the provisions of the standard general conditions that relate to the contractor's responsibilities.

The answer is C.

103. If a general contractor fails to pay a subcontractor, the subcontractor can protect its financial interests by using

    A. a performance bond
    B. a contractor's affidavit of payment
    C. builder's risk insurance
    D. a mechanic's lien

Solution

A *mechanic's lien* is a claim by one party against the property of another party for the satisfaction of a debt. It can be used by a material supplier, subcontractor, or contractor who has a financial interest in the project to gain payment. In some states, the architect can file a mechanic's lien to obtain payment for professional services rendered. In extreme cases, a mechanic's lien can force the sale of the owner's property to satisfy the debt. A lien encumbers the owner's property, making it impossible to sell or transfer the property until the lien is satisfied. This is usually enough pressure to force the owner to resolve the situation.

> *Study Note:* As an alternative to liens, a labor and material payment bond can protect the owner against claims by subcontractors and suppliers who are not paid by the general contractor. The bond gives these parties the right to collect payment from the surety (the company that issued the bond).
>
> Review and understand the various types of bonds used on a construction project, including a bid bond, a performance bond, and a labor and material payment bond. Also understand the different types of insurance and how insurance differs from a bond.

The answer is D.

104. According to AIA Document B141, *Standard Form of Agreement Between Owner and Architect* (RAIC Document 6), the architect must prepare cost estimates for the project during the

    A. schematic design phase
    B. design development phase
    C. schematic and design development phases
    D. schematic, design development, and construction documents phases

Solution

AIA Document B141 (RAIC Document 6) requires the architect to develop a preliminary cost estimate based on area, volume, or a similar conceptual estimating technique, and subsequently update it at each phase through to the construction documents phase.

> *Study Note:* Know the different types of estimating used for the various phases of design.

The answer is D.

105. When deciding on the types and amounts of insurance needed for a project, which of the following sources should the owner rely on?

I.   architect
II. contractor
III. owner's attorney
IV. owner's insurance agent

    A. I only
    B. I and IV only
    C. II and III only
    D. III and IV only

Solution

The owner should seek advice from his or her legal counsel and insurance agent on matters of insurance.

The architect should not give insurance advice. The architect can assist the owner and insurance agent by providing AIA Document G612, *Owner's Instructions Regarding the Construction Contract, Insurance and Bonds, and Bidding* (CCDC 21, *A Guide to Construction Insurance*). The contractor should only be involved with the various types of insurance that contractors must carry for the project.

> *Study Note:* Review the various provisions and requirements for insurance in Article 11 in AIA Document A201 (or the appropriate sections of CCAC Document 2).

The answer is D.

106. According to AIA Document A101 (CCDC Document 2), the owner's final payment must be made

    A. no later than 30 days after issuance of the final certificate for payment
    B. no later than 30 days following substantial completion (substantial performance)
    C. upon approval by the architect following correction of final punch list items
    D. within 30 days following issuance of the certificate of occupancy

Solution

Article 5 of AIA Document A101 (CCDC Document 2) states that final payment to the contractor shall be made no later than 30 days after the issuance of the architect's final certificate for payment, unless other provisions are written in.

Study Note: Review the owner-contractor agreements (AIA Documents A201 and A101, CCDC Document 2) and understand the basic provisions, including beginning dates of construction, substantial completion, liquidated damages, and payment processes.

The answer is A.

107. On a large, privately funded project, the lowest bid is 5% higher than the owner's original budget. Under the provisions of AIA Document B141 (RAIC Document 6), the owner elects to revise the project scope and quality to reduce the cost. In this case the architect must

    A. proceed to reduce the project scope and quality on a time and materials basis

    B. develop an addendum to the owner-architect agreement for additional services

    C. work with the owner to revise the project with additional compensation

    D. modify the contract documents as necessary, without additional compensation, to comply with the budget

Solution

Article 2.1.7 of AIA Document B141 (RAIC Document 6) requires that the architect shall, without additional compensation, modify the documents for which the architect is responsible as necessary to comply with the budget.

Study Note: Under the same article, the architect is entitled to compensation for all services performed, even if the owner elects to terminate the agreement and not build the project. Additionally, the architect does not warrant or represent that bids or negotiated prices will not vary from the owner's budget or from any estimate of the cost of the work prepared or agreed to by the architect.

The answer is D.

108. Under the provisions of AIA Document B141 (RAIC Document 6), the architect is NOT required to

    A. review laws and regulations applicable to the project

    B. commission tests for possible groundwater pollution

    C. develop a schedule of performance for architectural services

    D. name a designated representative to act on the architect's behalf

Solution

Article 1.2.2 of AIA Document B141 (RAIC Document 6) clearly states that one of the responsibilities of the owner is to furnish tests, inspections, and reports required by law or by the contract documents. These include structural, mechanical, and chemical tests for air and water pollution or for hazardous materials.

The answer is B.

109. For the remodeling and renovation of a historic building, the architect retains the services of a historic preservation consultant using AIA Document C141, *Standard Form of Agreement Between Architect and Consultant* (RAIC Document 9). The consultant's services include developing drawings showing the repair and anchoring of existing stonework. During construction the contractor discovers that the anchoring methods specified by the consultant violate the local building code and have to be modified at additional cost. The party responsible for the cost of the modifications is the

    A. architect

    B. consultant

    C. contractor

    D. owner

Solution

Under the provisions of AIA Document C141 (RAIC Document 9), consultants are responsible for code compliance regarding their area of work and for the accurate production of their drawings.

The answer is B.

110. Prior to the commencement of design work, furnishing a site survey is the responsibility of the

    A. architect
    B. civil engineer
    C. contractor
    D. owner

Solution

The owner is required to furnish and pay for site surveys according to both AIA Document B141 and AIA Document A201 (RAIC Document 6 and CCDC Document 2).

The answer is D.

111. During design development for a small corporate headquarters building, the client informs the architect that the estimated construction costs must be reduced. Which three of the following actions would most likely reduce these costs?

I. Design and specify larger tolerances.
II. Examine areas of high maintenance and improve their quality.
III. Suggest changes that would make custom details closer to industry standards.
IV. Examine ways to reduce the number of pieces in the details.
V. Try to reduce the number of different details involved in the project.

    A. I, II, and IV
    B. I, III, and V
    C. II, III, and IV
    D. III, IV, and V

Solution

Using industry standard details, reducing the number of components in the construction assembly, and reducing the number of unique details would all help reduce construction costs. There is not enough information given to determine if tolerances smaller than industry standards have been specified. Simply increasing tolerances greater than normal will not decrease the cost because contractors will price standard tolerances unless there is reason to do otherwise.

Although it is implied that life-cycle costs are a consideration because this is a corporate headquarters (presumably owner occupied and maintained), the question clearly states that "estimated construction costs" should be reduced, which means initial costs.

The answer is D.

112. According to AIA Document B141 (RAIC Document 6), which of the following services is NOT part of the architect's basic services for project closeout?

    A. forwarding written warranties to the owner
    B. sending a consent of surety to the owner
    C. providing start-up assistance
    D. meeting with the owner to determine the need for facility operation services

Solution

Article 2.8.3 of AIA Document B141 (RAIC Document 6) lists services that the architect will provide only if specifically designated. Start-up assistance is one of these services.

Study Note: Review the list of extra services that are not normally part of the architect's standard services. These include, among others, programming, geotechnical services, existing facilities surveys, site analysis, landscape design, interior design, detailed cost estimating, on-site project representation, record drawings, and post-contract evaluation.

The answer is C.

113. What is one way an architect can ensure that the client's design goals will be satisfied by the final set of construction documents?

    A. Meet periodically with the project designer, job captain, and programmer to compare the current status of the construction drawings with schematic design documents.
    B. Have another architect in the office who is not working on the project review the drawings for compliance with the original program report.
    C. Send the client periodic check sets of drawings, and request that any corrections be communicated to the architect's office within a set time period.
    D. Make a checklist of design requirements based on the original design goals, and give this to the people working on the job so that they have a constant reminder of the client's needs.

Solution

Meeting regularly with the people responsible for the programming, design, and execution of the project is the best way to facilitate communication.

Having another architect look at the drawings may be a good way to do a technical check, but that person may not be aware of the client's design goals. It is common to request from the client information necessary to design the project and complete the working drawings, but isolating the client in reviewing them (unless specifically requested) does not encourage an exchange of ideas and information. Some clients are not savvy enough to understand the drawings or may feel uncomfortable asking questions, so issues may go unaddressed. Making a checklist for the drafting staff is a good way to communicate project goals to the team, but realization of the client's objectives will require more coordination than a checklist will allow.

The answer is A.

114. Which type of architectural services fee structure is preferable when a client is embarking on his or her first architectural project and does not yet have a program?

- A. fixed sum
- B. multiple of direct personnel expense
- C. percentage of construction cost
- D. unit cost based on square footage

Solution

It is very likely that clients undertaking their first construction project without a program would spend a great deal of their time and the architect's time determining needs and making decisions. Programming is not considered to be part of the architect's basic services. A cost plus fee method such as *multiple of direct personnel expense* would ensure that no matter how much time was spent on the project, the architect would still cover expenses and make a profit.

The answer is B.

115. A client owns a large manufacturing plant and needs to expand to a new facility quickly and without interruption in production. The owner has arranged for a flexible line of credit to finance construction and wants to minimize project costs. The new facility will be very similar to the previous one, but sized for greater production capacity. Which type of construction delivery method should be recommended?

- A. design-build
- B. fast-track
- C. multiple prime contract
- D. design-award-build

Solution

The *fast-track* method would help keep costs down and be appropriate for a client who must move to a new facility as soon as possible. In this situation, it is likely that the owner

is familiar with the construction process, knows what is needed in this particular building, and would be comfortable with allowing some construction to proceed before the design was finalized. A disadvantage to the fast-track method of construction delivery is that the final cost of the work is often undetermined at the start of construction. However, with a flexible line of credit, a fixed price upfront would not be as important as with some other methods of financing.

The answer is B.

116. Which of the following is NOT an accurate statement?

- A. The architect is responsible for a defect in the work if he or she sees the defect during a site visit but fails to report it to the contractor.
- B. The owner has the sole right to make changes in the work but must do so through the architect.
- C. The architect does not have to verify soil test reports given by the owner.
- D. When the construction documents are almost complete, the architect must update the preliminary estimate of the cost of the work.

Solution

The architect has a duty and ethical responsibility to keep the contractor informed of any nonconforming work and to cooperate in getting the job done, but may not be held legally responsible. AIA Document A201 states that the contractor will not be relieved of obligations to perform the work in accordance with the contract documents by activities or duties of the architect. It also states that if the contractor performs any construction activity knowing it involves an error, the contractor will assume responsibility.

The answer is A.

117. Which of the following need NOT be proven before an architect can be found negligent?

- A. The architect had a duty toward the other party.
- B. The architect violated a written contractual agreement.
- C. The architect committed a breach of duty.
- D. The damage was caused by a breach of duty on the part of the architect.

Solution

Duty need not be established by a written agreement, although this is most often the case. Duty can arise based on the actions of the architect.

The answer is B.

118. The form of business organization that is best suited to minimizing the individual liability of its owners is the

    A. general partnership
    B. joint venture
    C. limited liability company
    D. limited partnership

Solution

The business organization best suited to minimize the individual liability of its owners is the *limited liability company*.

General partners bear responsibility for the actions of the other partners and their personal assets are vulnerable. A joint venture simply refers to how two or more offices temporarily organize to complete a project. The individual offices may be organized in any form, including a sole proprietorship. In a limited partnership, the general partners (owners) are still financially responsible, as with the general partnership. The limited partners only have liability to the extent of their investment, but they do not take part in the management of the company.

The answer is C.

119. The architect can best chart the involvement and responsibilities of all members of the project team with a

    A. flow diagram meeting
    B. full wall schedule
    C. Gantt chart
    D. project monitoring chart

Solution

The *full wall schedule* technique requires everyone on the project to work on developing the project schedule. This facilitates discussion about work tasks, responsibilities, and project deadlines. Participation of all team members is encouraged, and as a result everyone has a vested interest in the final schedule.

The answer is B.

120. A tort may arise from

    A. criminal activity of the architect
    B. unauthorized downloading of software
    C. negligence of the architect
    D. theft by an employee of an architect

Solution

A *tort* is a civil wrong resulting from negligence as opposed to a criminal act. The other three choices are criminal acts.

The answer is C.

121. Which of the following is NOT an advantage of a sole proprietorship?

    A. ease of establishment
    B. liability is limited to the owner's investment
    C. management control by the owner
    D. tax advantages

Solution

A sole proprietor has unlimited liability for negligence or other claims against the company, and is subject to claims on personal property and other assets.

The answer is B.

122. About one-third of the way through development of construction documents, a project architect notices that fee expenditures are about 15% over budget. What is the first course of action the architect should take to ensure the project makes a profit?

    A. Determine what has caused the problem.
    B. Notify the client that fees may need to be increased.
    C. Alert the firm owners, and ask for direction to correct the problem.
    D. Modify the remainder of the project schedule and fee allocation.

Solution

Determining the cause of the problem should be the first step in reining in project fees. It may be that the client is indecisive or asking for work beyond the original scope of services. Personnel may be spending time developing unnecessary details. It may be possible to assign tasks to employees with lower billing rates to keep costs under control. In any event, this course of action would be a first step before the firm's owners are notified, because they would want to know the cause of the problem.

The remainder of the design schedule may have to be modified, but only after the root cause of the original problem is determined. If the problem was caused by the architectural firm, the client should not be asked for more money. However, if the client is requesting work beyond the original scope, the firm may be entitled to fees for additional services.

The answer is A.

123. At the beginning of a project the owner asks the architect to recommend the types of insurance the owner will need to carry for the duration of the project. Which of the following responses would be appropriate? (Choose the two that apply.)

    A. Give the owner AIA Document G612 (CCDC Document 21).

    B. Suggest the standard insurance types, and advise the owner about optional insurance.

    C. Tell the owner that the owner's insurance agent should make the recommendations.

    D. Arrange a meeting with the architect's insurance counselor and the owner.

    E. Call the owner's insurance agent and tell him what the owner needs.

    F. Refer to AIA Document A201(CCDC Document 2) for a list of required insurances.

Solution

An architect is not authorized to give insurance advice. The architect should inform the owner that insurance decisions should be made in consultation with the owner's insurance or legal advisors. He or she may provide AIA Document G612, *Owner's Instructions Regarding the Construction Contract, Insurance and Bonds, and Bidding* (CCDC Document 21, *A Guide to Construction Insurance*) as a guide.

The answer is A and C.

124. Monitoring architectural fees and percentage of project completion is most often done

    A. daily

    B. weekly

    C. biweekly

    D. monthly

Solution

Most projects, large or small, are monitored on a weekly basis. This provides the opportunity to catch problems early enough to take corrective action and fits into the normal weekly cycle of office management, allowing employee assignments and deadlines to be made according to the project's status and the status of other work in the office.

Daily management would require too much time and would not give a broad enough view of the project as it progresses. Biweekly monitoring could be done for very large and lengthy jobs, but it might not allow corrections of problems to be made in time to be most effective. Monitoring on a monthly basis would definitely allow problems to grow before being discovered.

The answer is B.

125. The office organizational structure that would give individual employees the most job satisfaction is

    A. departmental

    B. pyramidal

    C. sole proprietorship

    D. studio

Solution

The *studio* format of office organization gives individual employees the most job satisfaction.

A *departmental* structure often pigeonholes employees into doing only one type of job or task. While some employees like this, most architects and intern architects like variety. A *pyramidal* organization is a "top-down" type of structure where the principal makes decisions and hands off the work to subordinates who do not have the opportunity to get involved in all aspects of a business. Most *sole proprietorships* are small businesses where individual employees often get to do a variety of types of work but decisions regarding assignments are the purview of the principal.

The answer is D.

126. Which project best demonstrates the influence of the architect's structural engineering consultants on the overall design?

    A. Chrysler Building, William Van Alen, New York, 1930

    B. Sears Tower, Bruce Graham (Skidmore, Owings & Merrill), Chicago, 1973

    C. AT&T Building, Philip Johnson & John Burgee, New York, 1978

    D. Guggenheim Museum, Frank Gehry, Bilbao, Spain, 1997

Solution

The Sears Tower in Chicago is a good example of how the influence of structural engineers can enhance the design of a building. Similarly, mechanical or electrical engineers may have a great impact on the appearance of a structure, particularly if they have designed elements that take advantage of natural heating and cooling techniques and daylighting.

The answer is B.

127. An architecture firm is establishing billing rates for employees working on a large hotel project. The firm plans to propose a cost plus fee compensation method. Which of the following criteria would NOT be factored into the calculation of each employee's billing rate?

- A. a percentage of the construction cost
- B. direct salaries of employees
- C. cost of benefits such as insurance and vacation time
- D. taxes

Solution

There are a variety of compensation methods architects can propose when negotiating with a potential client. The most common methods are fixed fees, cost plus fees, percentage of construction cost, and unit costs.

The *cost plus fee method* compensates the architect for the actual cost of doing the work plus a fee for profit. Fees are generally billed at hourly rates, determined as a multiple of a person's salary or salary plus benefits. The multiplier is adjusted based on overhead the firm must pay and profit levels the firm wishes to achieve; generally multipliers range from 2 to 3.5. Calculations of appropriate billing rates must consider the person's base salary, any benefits offered to that employee, and taxes.

A *fixed fee* is a stipulated sum of money that the client will pay the architect for services. The services are agreed upon in advance, and changes to the services made by the owner generally warrant additional compensation for the architect. The fees are determined by creating a list of tasks necessary to complete the project, assigning hours and personnel to each task, and multiplying the number of hours expected to complete the task by each person's hourly billing rate. The result is a ballpark fee based upon the personnel selected and the time the estimator thinks that it will take to complete the project. The estimate can then be adjusted to arrive at a fee that the estimator believes will allow the firm to make a profit on the project. If the estimator guesses incorrectly and it actually takes more time to complete the work, the firm may have to absorb the extra expenses.

The *percentage of construction cost fee* structure is not commonly used today. With this method, the professional's fee is a percentage of the cost of project construction. However, with this method a client may wonder if the architect will design a more expensive project to increase the design fee, or conversely, a relatively inexpensive project may be very complicated and the percentage of construction cost may not cover the architect's expenses to design the project.

The *unit cost* method bases fees upon some unit, such as square footage. This fee structure is sometimes used for projects such as a tenant space fit-out, where the scope of the work is relatively similar from one project to another.

The answer is A.

128. AIA Document G612, *Owner's Instructions to the Architect Regarding the Construction Contract*, is a checklist that owners can use to define project requirements as they relate to the general conditions. This form requests that the owner consult with legal and insurance counsel to discuss issues that will be addressed in the supplementary conditions and in the contract documents. This form does NOT request information about

- A. liability insurance requirements
- B. design schedule
- C. method of procurement
- D. equal opportunity requirements

Solution

The questions posed in AIA Document G612, *Owner's Instructions to the Architect Regarding the Construction Contract*, deal with the owner-contractor contract. This checklist provides a guide for the owner and the owner's attorney and insurance agent as they establish the requirements for a particular project and develop the specific language used to modify the contract. The architect may also furnish AIA Document A503, *Guide for Supplementary Conditions*, to further assist the owner and the owner's counsel in writing the supplementary conditions. Note that drafting the supplementary conditions is the responsibility of the owner.

As the design schedule is a matter of coordination between the architect and the owner, schedules and other design requirements are detailed in the first part of AIA Document B141, *Standard Form of Agreement Between Owner and Architect*.

The answer is B.

BUILDING SECTION VIGNETTE

Directions

Draw a building section corresponding to the section cut line on the plans for a two-story building, shown on the following page. Include the exterior walls, foundation, interior partitions, finished ceilings, structural elements, HVAC equipment, and anything else that is cut by the cut line as well as joists in elevation immediately adjacent to the cut line. The section must accurately reflect the dimensions and spatial relations given in the program and on the plans. Vertical spacing not explicitly stated in the program must be accurately interpreted and indicated on the section.

Program

The structural system for this vignette consists of top-chord bearing steel joists on masonry bearing walls with continuous concrete spread footings and a 6 in (152) concrete slab on grade.

1. All ceilings and roofs are flat with a 4 in (100) concrete slab on the joists.

2. The ceiling height of the lounge is 17 ft 0 in (5180). The ceiling height of the other first- and second-floor spaces is 8 ft 6 in (2590).

3. The space between each ceiling and floor or roof slab must be held to the minimum dimension required to accommodate light fixtures and the mechanical and structural components shown on the plans.

4. All ducts must be placed below the joists.

5. Provide 12 in (305) of clearance between the bottoms of the ducts and the finished ceiling to accommodate light fixtures and sprinkler pipes. Light fixtures need not be shown.

6. Ceiling spaces must be used as return air plenums.

7. The frost depth is 3 ft 6 in (1067) below grade.

8. Parapets must extend 2 ft 6 in (760) above the surface of decks at roof edges and at changes in the roof deck elevation.

9. Corridor walls must have a 1-hour (minimum) fire-resistance rating.

10. The site is level.

11. Footings are to be 1 ft (305) by 3 ft (914).

Tips

- Become familiar with each floor plan by turning the layers on and off.

- It may be useful to start by laying out a rough drawing and adjusting individual elements later.

- Use the *move group* tool to relocate an entire joist run. Use the *move, adjust* tool to change the location of the joists within the joist run.

- Zoom in frequently to make fine adjustments to element locations.

- If one element of two overlapping elements cannot be selected, keep clicking without moving the mouse until the desired element is highlighted.

Warnings

- A grade line *must* be drawn in order for the solution to be graded.

Tools

Useful tools include the following.

- layers to turn elements on and off in order to view the base drawings more clearly

- *zoom* tool for drawing and adjusting individual elements

- *sketch line* tool for establishing heights and clearances

- full-screen cursor to help align elements

Target Time: 1 hour

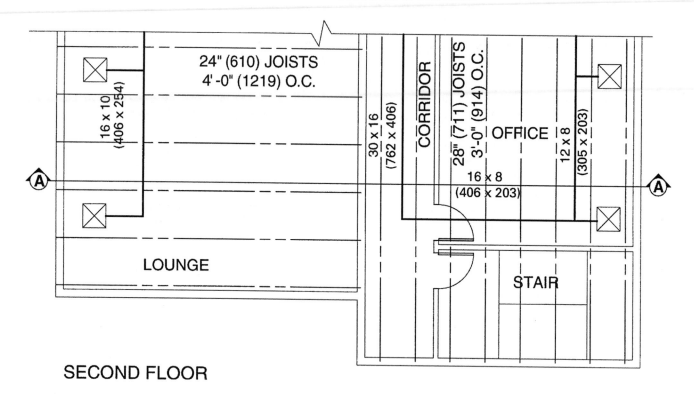

SECOND FLOOR

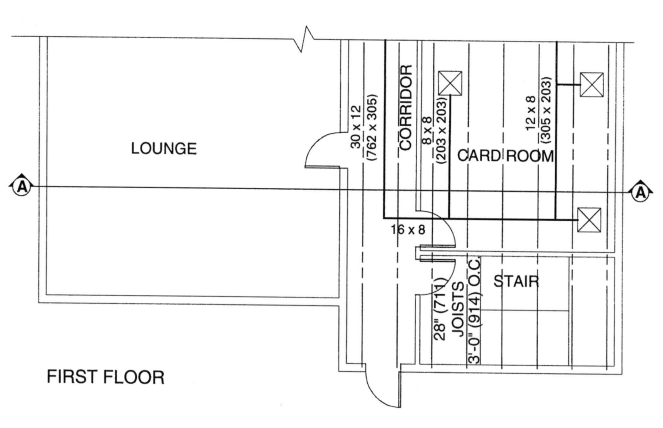

FIRST FLOOR

Scale: 1/8" = 1'-0"
(1:100 metric)

BUILDING SECTION

BUILDING SECTION: SOLVING APPROACH

Completing this vignette successfully depends on careful reading of the program. Read through the instructions a couple of times and take notes if it will be helpful. All the information necessary to solve this problem is given in the instructions. Pay particular attention to the location of the section cut line and note anything it intersects, including exterior walls, windows, rated partitions, ductwork, joists, beams, and doors. All the elements the cut line intersects *must* show up on the building section.

It's easiest to make sure things align by drawing the section over the floor plan, using the cut line as the datum.

Start at grade. The program for this vignette indicates that the site is flat, which can be represented with a horizontal line. Make sure the line extends the whole way across the building section, beyond the exterior walls on either side.

Next, locate the bearing walls. (They are generally drawn thicker on the floor plan than partition walls.) The plan will indicate the wall thickness. The program states that the masonry bearing walls have continuous concrete spread footings that are 1 ft by 3 ft (305 by 914). Center each footing under the wall. Place the *tops* (not bottoms) of the exterior footings at the frost depth of 3 ft 6 in (1067) below grade given in the program. This gives a margin of error because the bottoms of the exterior footings must be no higher than the frost line. Footings under interior walls can be placed directly below the slab.

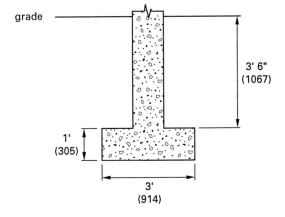

The program states that the slab is 6 in (152) thick and *on grade.*

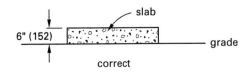

correct

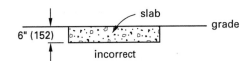

incorrect

Next, determine the vertical dimensions required and begin laying out the vertical elements.

No structural or mechanical information is given at the area of the lobby on the first-floor plan, so it can be concluded that this is a double height space. The program states that the ceiling height in this area is 17 ft 0 in (5180). The second floor plan of the lobby area shows that the roof structure is composed of 24 in (610) joists at 4 ft 0 in (1219) on center. A 16 in × 10 in (406 × 254) duct runs below the structure, and the program requires 12 in (305) of clearance between the bottom of the ducts and the ceiling.

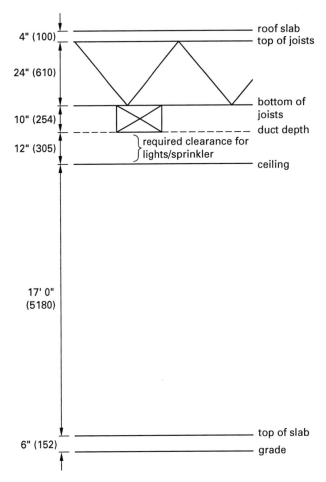

The east side of the building is a two-story space. Follow the same procedure to determine the vertical dimensions required. The deepest duct on each floor determines the required depth of the space allowed for mechanical equipment. (It is not always one of the ducts that intersects the section cut line, so look carefully.) On the first floor, the deepest duct is the 30 in × 12 in (762 × 305) duct in the corridor. On the second floor, it is the 30 in × 16 in (762 × 406) duct in the corridor.

After the vertical dimensions are established, draw in the details, such as joists at the proper spacing (or in elevation, if applicable) and duct sizes. The floor plan shows the duct runs diagrammatically with a single line; center the duct on this line.

Next, draw the interior partitions. If the program states that the walls are to be rated, they must extend from the floor slab to the bottom of the floor/ceiling deck above.

If the program calls for parapets, ensure that the bearing walls extend the proper height above the surface of the ceiling deck.

When the section is finished, check all dimensions, required clearances, and spacing against the program one final time.

BUILDING SECTION: PASSING SOLUTION

All the program requirements have been successfully met by this solution. Ducts where the section cut occurs have been drawn to the correct size, ceiling heights are correctly shown, and the structural members have been indicated correctly and in the proper positions. The foundations and parapets are also shown correctly. Rated partitions at the corridors extend from slab to slab.

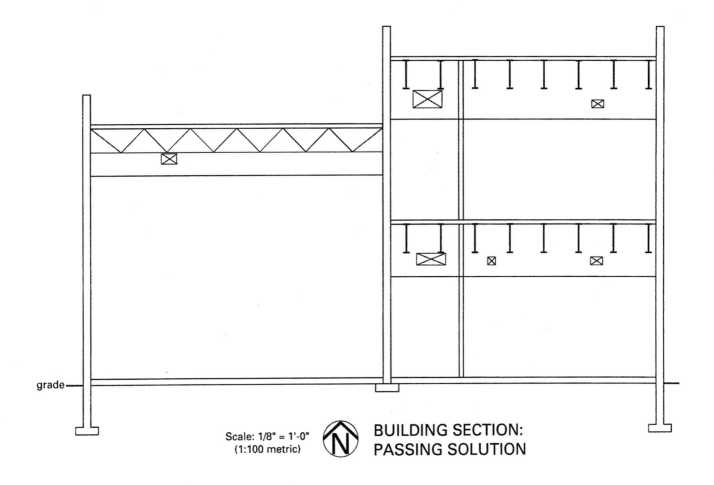

grade

Scale: 1/8" = 1'-0"
(1:100 metric)

BUILDING SECTION:
PASSING SOLUTION

BUILDING SECTION: FAILING SOLUTION

This solution has several faults. The interior footing is shown too low. Because it is an interior footing, it does not have to be at frost depth as the exterior footings do. The interior bearing wall should rest directly on the footing. The corridor partitions do not extend to the deck above on both the first and second floors as they must to create a fire-rated partition. On the first floor the 8 in × 8 in (200 × 200) duct is drawn too large. On the second floor there is not enough room below the large duct for light fixtures. The parapet at the interior bearing wall is shown incorrectly.

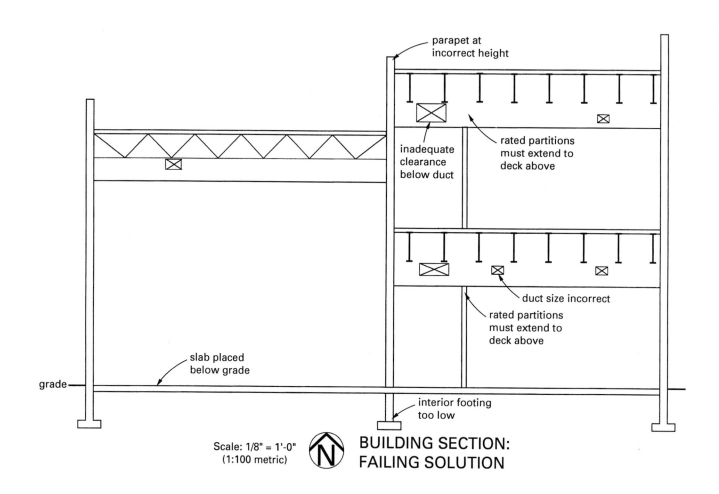

parapet at
incorrect height

inadequate
clearance
below duct

rated partitions
must extend to
deck above

duct size incorrect

rated partitions
must extend to
deck above

slab placed
below grade

grade

interior footing
too low

Scale: 1/8" = 1'-0"
(1:100 metric)

BUILDING SECTION:
FAILING SOLUTION

PRACTICE EXAM: MULTIPLE CHOICE

Directions

Reference books should not be used on this practice exam. Besides this book, you should have only a calculator, pencils, and scratch paper. (On the actual exam, these will be provided and should not be brought into the site.)

Target Time: 2 hours

1.	Ⓐ Ⓑ Ⓒ Ⓓ	26.	Ⓐ Ⓑ Ⓒ Ⓓ	51.	Ⓐ Ⓑ Ⓒ Ⓓ
✓2.	Ⓐ Ⓑ Ⓒ Ⓓ	27.	_____	52.	Ⓐ Ⓑ Ⓒ Ⓓ
3.	Ⓐ Ⓑ Ⓒ Ⓓ	28.	Ⓐ Ⓑ Ⓒ Ⓓ	53.	Ⓐ Ⓑ Ⓒ Ⓓ
4.	Ⓐ Ⓑ Ⓒ Ⓓ Ⓔ Ⓕ	29.	Ⓐ Ⓑ Ⓒ Ⓓ	54.	Ⓐ Ⓑ Ⓒ Ⓓ
5.	Ⓐ Ⓑ Ⓒ Ⓓ	30.	Ⓐ Ⓑ Ⓒ Ⓓ	55.	Ⓐ Ⓑ Ⓒ Ⓓ
6.	Ⓐ Ⓑ Ⓒ Ⓓ	31.	Ⓐ Ⓑ Ⓒ Ⓓ	56.	Ⓐ Ⓑ Ⓒ Ⓓ
✓7.	Ⓐ Ⓑ Ⓒ Ⓓ	32.	Ⓐ Ⓑ Ⓒ Ⓓ Ⓔ Ⓕ	57.	Ⓐ Ⓑ Ⓒ Ⓓ
8.	Ⓐ Ⓑ Ⓒ Ⓓ	33.	Ⓐ Ⓑ Ⓒ Ⓓ	58.	Ⓐ Ⓑ Ⓒ Ⓓ
9.	Ⓐ Ⓑ Ⓒ Ⓓ	34.	Ⓐ Ⓑ Ⓒ Ⓓ	59.	Ⓐ Ⓑ Ⓒ Ⓓ
10.	Ⓐ Ⓑ Ⓒ Ⓓ	35.	Ⓐ Ⓑ Ⓒ Ⓓ	60.	Ⓐ Ⓑ Ⓒ Ⓓ
✓11.	Ⓐ Ⓑ Ⓒ Ⓓ	36.	Ⓐ Ⓑ Ⓒ Ⓓ	61.	Ⓐ Ⓑ Ⓒ Ⓓ
12.	Ⓐ Ⓑ Ⓒ Ⓓ	37.	Ⓐ Ⓑ Ⓒ Ⓓ Ⓔ Ⓕ	62.	Ⓐ Ⓑ Ⓒ Ⓓ
✓13.	Ⓐ Ⓑ Ⓒ Ⓓ	38.	Ⓐ Ⓑ Ⓒ Ⓓ	63.	Ⓐ Ⓑ Ⓒ Ⓓ
✓14.	Ⓐ Ⓑ Ⓒ Ⓓ	39.	Ⓐ Ⓑ Ⓒ Ⓓ	64.	Ⓐ Ⓑ Ⓒ Ⓓ
15.	Ⓐ Ⓑ Ⓒ Ⓓ	40.	Ⓐ Ⓑ Ⓒ Ⓓ	65.	Ⓐ Ⓑ Ⓒ Ⓓ
✓16.	Ⓐ Ⓑ Ⓒ Ⓓ	41.	Ⓐ Ⓑ Ⓒ Ⓓ	66.	Ⓐ Ⓑ Ⓒ Ⓓ
✓17.	Ⓐ Ⓑ Ⓒ Ⓓ	42.	Ⓐ Ⓑ Ⓒ Ⓓ	67.	Ⓐ Ⓑ Ⓒ Ⓓ
✓18.	Ⓐ Ⓑ Ⓒ Ⓓ	43.	Ⓐ Ⓑ Ⓒ Ⓓ	68.	Ⓐ Ⓑ Ⓒ Ⓓ
✓19.	Ⓐ Ⓑ Ⓒ Ⓓ	44.	Ⓐ Ⓑ Ⓒ Ⓓ	69.	Ⓐ Ⓑ Ⓒ Ⓓ
20.	Ⓐ Ⓑ Ⓒ Ⓓ	45.	Ⓐ Ⓑ Ⓒ Ⓓ	70.	Ⓐ Ⓑ Ⓒ Ⓓ
21.	Ⓐ Ⓑ Ⓒ Ⓓ	46.	Ⓐ Ⓑ Ⓒ Ⓓ	71.	Ⓐ Ⓑ Ⓒ Ⓓ
22.	Ⓐ Ⓑ Ⓒ Ⓓ	47.	Ⓐ Ⓑ Ⓒ Ⓓ Ⓔ Ⓕ	72.	Ⓐ Ⓑ Ⓒ Ⓓ
23.	Ⓐ Ⓑ Ⓒ Ⓓ	48.	Ⓐ Ⓑ Ⓒ Ⓓ	73.	Ⓐ Ⓑ Ⓒ Ⓓ
24.	Ⓐ Ⓑ Ⓒ Ⓓ	49.	Ⓐ Ⓑ Ⓒ Ⓓ	74.	Ⓐ Ⓑ Ⓒ Ⓓ
25.	Ⓐ Ⓑ Ⓒ Ⓓ	50.	Ⓐ Ⓑ Ⓒ Ⓓ	75.	_____

76. Ⓐ Ⓑ Ⓒ Ⓓ
77. Ⓐ Ⓑ Ⓒ Ⓓ
78. Ⓐ Ⓑ Ⓒ Ⓓ
79. Ⓐ Ⓑ Ⓒ Ⓓ
80. Ⓐ Ⓑ Ⓒ Ⓓ
81. Ⓐ Ⓑ Ⓒ Ⓓ
82. Ⓐ Ⓑ Ⓒ Ⓓ
83. Ⓐ Ⓑ Ⓒ Ⓓ
84. Ⓐ Ⓑ Ⓒ Ⓓ
85. Ⓐ Ⓑ Ⓒ Ⓓ
86. Ⓐ Ⓑ Ⓒ Ⓓ
87. Ⓐ Ⓑ Ⓒ Ⓓ
88. Ⓐ Ⓑ Ⓒ Ⓓ
89. Ⓐ Ⓑ Ⓒ Ⓓ

90. Ⓐ Ⓑ Ⓒ Ⓓ
91. Ⓐ Ⓑ Ⓒ Ⓓ
92. Ⓐ Ⓑ Ⓒ Ⓓ
93. Ⓐ Ⓑ Ⓒ Ⓓ
94. Ⓐ Ⓑ Ⓒ Ⓓ
95. Ⓐ Ⓑ Ⓒ Ⓓ
96. Ⓐ Ⓑ Ⓒ Ⓓ
97. Ⓐ Ⓑ Ⓒ Ⓓ
98. Ⓐ Ⓑ Ⓒ Ⓓ
99. Ⓐ Ⓑ Ⓒ Ⓓ
100. Ⓐ Ⓑ Ⓒ Ⓓ

1. Which series of AIA Contract Documents would include a joint venture agreement between two architecture firms?

    A. A-series
    B. B-series
    C. C-series
    D. D-series

2. An architecture firm is facing a deadline on a large library project and decides to hire a freelance CAD drafter to assist the firm in completing the construction documents on time. According to the NCARB Rules of Conduct, what must the architect of record do to sign and seal the final drawings?

    A. The architect must redline the drawings and have the drafter make the appropriate corrections.
    B. The architect must review and correct the work after it is prepared by the drafter and incorporate it into the construction documents.
    C. The architect must thoroughly examine the drawings prepared by the drafter and incorporate the work into the construction documents. The firm must also retain documentation of communications with the drafter throughout his or her involvement with the project and must keep records of the architect's coordination of the work for five years.
    D. The architect may be subject to disciplinary action from the state registration board if he or she signs and seals the drawings, as this is not permissible.

3. AIA Document A201 requires the owner to purchase and maintain all these types of insurance EXCEPT

    A. all-risk property insurance
    B. boiler and machinery insurance
    C. project management protective liability insurance
    D. liability insurance

4. Which of the following types of business organization limit an individual's liability to the amount he or she has invested in the company? (Choose the three that apply.)

    A   a partnership
    B. a corporation
    C. a sole proprietorship
    D. a limited-liability company
    E. a limited-liability partnership
    F. a disadvantaged business enterprise

5. Contract documents form the basis of the legal relationship between the

    A. owner and architect
    B. contractor and subcontractor
    C. architect and contractor
    D. owner and contractor

6. An amount of money withheld from each application for payment is known as

    A. retainage
    B. deduction
    C. overhead
    D. liquidated damages

7. Which of the following need NOT be present to prove negligence?

    A. breach
    B. damage
    C. duty
    D. commission

8. A local code official would have the authority to enforce all of the following EXCEPT

    A. the Americans with Disabilities Act
    B. the Life Safety Code, NFPA 101
    C. the International Building Code
    D. ANSI A117.1

9. A cabinetry subcontractor drops off a box of counter-top material and hardware samples at an architect's office with a transmittal requesting selections by the end of the week. What should the architect do with the materials?

    A. Review the options and call the subcontractor with the selections.

    B. Review the options, make selections, and inform the contractor in writing of the choices.

    C. Send the samples back to the subcontractor.

    D. Send the samples to the contractor.

10. The architect has the authority to

    A. stop work

    B. reject work that does not comply with the construction documents

    C. order changes to the work that deduct from the contract sum

    D. accept nonconforming work

11. Which of the following items should NOT be addressed in the supplementary conditions?

    A. liquidated damages

    B. insurance requirements and limits

    C. administrative procedures

    D. legal requirements of the jurisdiction in which the project is located

12. The following are pages in a set of construction drawings for a small conference room renovation in a large office building. Arrange them in the correct order from the title sheet to the end of the set.

I. electrical and data plan

II. finish schedule

III. demolition and new work plans (on the same sheet)

IV. reflected ceiling plan

V. interior elevations

    A. III, IV, V, II, I

    B. I, III, V, IV, II

    C. II, V, III, I, IV

    D. III, I, IV, V, II

13. An architect writes a specification for floor tile for a public restroom, which states that the tile is to be "American Tile Company 12×12 porcelain floor tile, Pattern 463 Oceania, Color 42 Sandstorm or approved equal." The contractor contacts a local tile supplier and discovers that this product has a 12-week lead time, but it will be necessary to have the tile on site earlier to stay within the project schedule. If the contractor wishes to propose a different tile, when must that request to the architect be submitted?

    A. during preparation of submittals

    B. prior to preparing a bid

    C. after the contract is awarded and an agreement with the tiling subcontractor is signed

    D. during the project kick-off meeting

14. In which CSI MasterFormat™ 2004 division would a specification for glass block be found?

    A. Division 04

    B. Division 08

    C. Division 09

    D. Division 13

15. Which of the following is LEAST likely to be included in a submittal?

    A. shop drawings of a storefront window assembly

    B. MSDS for trowel-on block filler

    C. vinyl wall base samples

    D. cut sheets for a paper towel dispenser

16. A developer from New York owns a large piece of property along the James River in Virginia and plans to construct a retirement community and golf course. This is an area where there are many pockets of unstable shrink/swell soil, so the architect advises the owner to hire a geotechnical engineer to conduct testing and prepare a soils report for the property. The developer bids construction of the clubhouse and provides a copy of the soils report to each of the bidders along with the contract documents. The low bidder and the developer reach an agreement based upon AIA Document A201. Three weeks into the site excavation, the contractor finds areas of shrink/swell soil in locations not indicated in the soils report. Who is responsible for the cost of additional excavation and/or foundation design and reinforcement?

A. the contractor

B. the geotechnical engineer

C. the owner

D. the architect

17. At the completion of a project, the architect is NOT required to provide the owner with

A. a final certificate of payment

B. an occupancy permit

C. a consent of surety to release retainage and lien and bond waivers

D. warranties

18. Who is responsible for preparing a punch list?

A. the architect

B. the contractor

C. the owner

D. the architect, with the assistance of his consultants

19. A preliminary code evaluation of a project requires that the architect possess a certain amount of information about the proposed building. Which of the following is NOT a key piece of information in the initial step?

A. type of occupancy

B. means of egress

C. required type of fire suppression system

D. type of construction

20. A contractor is installing a colonnade at the perimeter of a dining courtyard in an open-air shopping mall. The drawings show 12 in (305) diameter columns spaced at 8 ft (2438) on center. However, the description in the millwork specification calls for 10 in (254) diameter Roman Doric columns. The contractor should

A. provide 12 in (305) diameter columns

B. provide 10 in (254) diameter columns

C. consult the owner

D. consult the architect

21. While removing floor tile in the lobby of an old theater, a contractor suspects that the mastic may contain asbestos. In accordance with AIA Document A201, she stops work and reports her findings to the owner. The owner hires a testing laboratory, which confirms the contractor's suspicions. The project is at a standstill for three weeks while abatement takes place. When the area is clear, the contractor prepares a change order request for a time extension and compensation for expenses incurred as a result of the discovery. The owner refuses, stating that the contractor's proposal for four extra weeks and $10,000 to cover shutdown and startup costs is unreasonable. What is the next step?

A. The architect should issue a construction change directive and order the work to proceed so that more time is not lost while the owner and contractor negotiate.

B. The claim should proceed directly to mediation.

C. Because the project was shut down for three weeks, the contract time should automatically be extended by three weeks.

D. The architect should review the claim and make a decision.

22. According to the NCARB Rules of Conduct, an architect's license or registration could be revoked if

I. a physical or mental disability impairs the architect's professional competence

II. in talking with a potential client, the architect fails to disclose ownership of stock in the client's chief competitor, and that personal financial interest may influence his or her judgment

III. in a television interview about a controversial casino project, the architect discloses that he or she is employed by the resort developer

IV. the architect pays for overnight accommodations and dinner for a potential client so that the client may visit the architect's firm for a second interview about a large project

A. II only

B. I and II only

C. I and IV only

D. II and III only

23. According to AIA Document A201,

    A. the architect must approve the contractor's construction schedule before work can begin

    B. the architect must approve the contractor's schedule of submittals

    C. the contractor is responsible for preparing record drawings

    D. the architect is responsible for reviewing all submittals provided by the contractor

24. Submittals should be required for which of the following?

I. granite countertops and transaction counters of a concierge desk in a luxury hotel

II. cherry stile and rail paneling in a law firm's conference room

III. steel framing system for a high-rise office building

IV. unfaced batt insulation, used as acoustical blankets above the ceiling and in the walls of a law firm's conference room

    A. I and II only

    B. II and III only

    C. I, II, and III only

    D. I, III, and IV only

25. Which of the following would be the LEAST legitimate reason for an architect to withhold all or part of a certificate for payment?

    A. There are mathematical errors on the contractor's application for payment, and the stated amount to be paid is higher than the actual sum of the line items.

    B. The architect has been notified by the owner that the plumbing subcontractor's attorney has notified him of the subcontractor's intent to place a lien on the project.

    C. The contractor has failed to correct a portion of the work that the architect has rejected.

    D. One month remains in the construction period on a project with $5000 liquidated damages per day, and the architect suspects that work will not be completed by the deadline; not enough unpaid funds remain to cover the liquidated damages for the expected delay.

26. The design occupant load of a hotel ballroom would be determined by

    A. drawing proposed layouts of the room for receptions, meetings, and dining, and figuring out how many chairs will fit into the space in each scenario

    B. dividing the total square footage of the space by a factor that allocates space for each person

    C. multiplying the number of people expected to use the space by an assumed weight per person

    D. asking the conference services manager how many people must be accommodated in the space

27. A design for a rest station at an amusement park includes a group of six family restrooms, each containing a toilet, lavatory, and changing table. At least _____ of these restrooms must be accessible. (Fill in the blank.)

28. An architect is working on a restaurant project with a brilliant but eccentric world-famous chef. The architect and owner have an agreement based upon AIA Document B141. Which of the following situations would NOT entitle the architect to an adjustment of schedule and fees?

    A. The architect is required to defend the owner's choice of sculpture and neon signage at several hearings of the city's architectural review board.

    B. The owner decides to bid the project rather than negotiate with a contractor.

    C. The chef often travels to a villa in Italy and cannot be reached for weeks at a time.

    D. The mechanical and electrical engineers, consultants to the architect, fail to coordinate the power and ventilation requirements for the walk-in cooler.

29. During the construction of a church, the building committee decides to replace the porcelain tile floor specified for the chapel with a poured terrazzo flooring material. The architect requests a proposal from the contractor for the change. The contract states that the contractor may add 20% for overhead and profit and an additional 5% for coordination on change orders. The contractor's base price for labor and materials for the change is $22,250. What is the approximate total value of the change order?

A. $26,700
B. $27,800
C. $28,000
D. $28,400

30. An architect should specify a mock-up for

I.   a CMU foundation wall for a small warehouse

II. kitchen cabinetry, granite countertops, and mosaic tile backsplashes for a series of identical apartments

III. a custom-designed carpet inlay in the lobby of a hotel

IV. a portion of a brick wall for an addition to a 1760s building

A. I and III only
B. II and III only
C. II and IV only
D. II, III, and IV only

31. Where does a measurement of exit access travel distance begin?

A. at a corridor wall
B. at a building exit
C. at the end of the common path of egress travel
D. at the most remote point within a space

32. A local volunteer fire company is planning construction of a new fire station. A limited amount of funding is available for the project, and the owner wishes to set a fixed limit of construction cost at $1.5 million. The architect agrees, and the parties sign AIA Document B141. The architect exercises his authority over the scope of the project and the materials specified to meet the budget, and his final cost projection for the project is just under the maximum price. However, when the bids are received, the lowest base bid is $10,000 over the fixed limit of construction cost. What are the owner's possible options? (Choose the four that apply.)

A. abandon the project and terminate the architect's contract

B. rebid the project

C. increase the budget and award the contract to the lowest bidder

D. require the architect to revise the drawings, with no additional compensation, to comply with the budget

E. require the architect to pay the difference between the cost projection and the low bid

F. require the architect to negotiate with the contractor to achieve a lower price

33. According to AIA Document A201, which of the following statements is FALSE?

A. The owner can require the contractor to name him or her as an additional insured on the contractor's liability insurance policy.

B. If the owner chooses not to purchase property insurance and does not notify the contractor of this decision, the owner becomes responsible for all losses that the property insurance would have covered.

C. If the owner requires the contractor to purchase project management protective liability insurance, it becomes the owner, contractor, and architect's primary vicarious liability insurance for construction operations under that contract.

D. The owner is responsible for paying property insurance deductibles.

34. Who can propose a change to the International Building Code?

A. only members of the International Code Council
B. only local code officials
C. only licensed design professionals
D. anyone

35. Bids are received for the addition of an early-childhood learning center and playground at an elementary school. The following bids are submitted.

bidder	base bid	bid alternate 1	bid alternate 2
ABC Construction	$244,150	$22,465	−$6725
Sunny Day, Inc.	$265,430	$15,846	−$5000
Grover and Sons	$270,000	$14,000	−$2000
B&E General Contractors	$246,765	$18,768	−$7500

The school district plans to accept both bid alternates. Which company would be awarded the contract?

A. ABC Construction
B. Sunny Day, Inc.
C. Grover and Sons
D. B&E General Contractors

36. Just inside the entrance at a major retail store is a small coffee shop. The total floor area of the coffee shop is 600 ft², which is much less than 10% of the floor area of the entire store. For the purposes of code evaluation, this space would be classified as

    A.   accessory
    B.   ancillary
    C.   assembly
    D.   an incidental use area

37. Which of these should be included in an advertisement to bid? (Choose the four that apply.)

    A.   the name and address of the architect
    B.   the date, time, and location of the pre-bid conference
    C.   the amount of deposit required for bidding documents
    D.   the names of acceptable subcontractors
    E.   bid forms
    F.   the date, time, and location at which bids are due

38. Identify the following graphic symbols for architectural drawings.

I.

II.

III.   ◇6

IV.   (101/A)

    A.   I-elevation, II-window type, III-revision, IV-door type
    B.   I-revision, II-window type, III-elevation, IV-door type
    C.   I-elevation, II-revision, III-door type, IV-window type
    D.   I-revision, II-elevation, III-window type, IV-door type

39. What type of drawings would contain finish floor heights, information about materials and types of construction assemblies, and window head heights?

    A.   floor plans
    B.   building sections
    C.   interior elevations
    D.   wall sections

40. What must architects do to protect their interest in the copyright on the instruments of service produced for a project and the design of a building?

    A.   register the drawings and photographs of the completed building with the U.S. Copyright Office
    B.   file a copy of the instruments of service in the Library of Congress
    C.   put the copyright symbol © and the date on the drawings
    D.   none of the above is required to protect the architect's copyright

41. Where does a common path of egress travel end?

    A.   in an area of refuge
    B.   at the exterior exit from the building
    C.   at the point where an individual has a choice about which direction to go to reach an exit
    D.   at a public way

42. Who prepares the owner-contractor agreement?

    A.   the architect, using standard AIA document forms or software
    B.   the owner, with the assistance of the architect
    C.   the owner's attorney
    D.   the contractor

43. A university is planning to build a new science center to house its chemistry and biology departments. The school wishes to encourage competitive bidding but also to ensure that the materials used meet a minimum standard of quality. Which type of specification should be used?

    A.   proprietary
    B.   base bid with "approved equal" language
    C.   descriptive
    D.   base bid with alternates

PRACTICE EXAM

49

44. "Vinyl composition tile shall be maintained at a minimum of 65°F (18°C) for 48 hours prior to installation, during installation, and for 48 hours after completion." In what part of the specification would the contractor find these instructions?

    A. Part I, General
    B. Part II, Products
    C. Part III, Execution
    D. Division 01, General Requirements

45. If a penalty clause is included in the owner-contractor agreement, what else must be included?

    A. liquidated damages
    B. guaranteed maximum price
    C. a bonus provision
    D. an incentive clause

46. An architecture firm is designing a tranquil, spa-like treatment center for cosmetic dentistry. The dental clinic will be housed within an existing building. The architect's scope of services includes space planning; detailing new partition walls; coordinating updates to the mechanical, electrical, data, and plumbing systems with appropriate consultants; providing interior design services; and selecting and procuring furnishings for the suite. Which AIA document or documents would be most appropriate for use as the owner-contractor agreements for this project?

    A. A101: *Owner-Contractor Agreement Form—Stipulated Sum,* with A201: *General Conditions of the Contract for Construction*
    B. A107: *Abbreviated Standard Form of Agreement Between Owner and Contractor for Construction Projects of Limited Scope, Stipulated Sum*
    C. A105: *Standard Form of Agreement Between Owner and Contractor for a Small Project,* with A205: *General Conditions of the Contract for Construction of a Small Project*
    D. A171: *Owner-Contractor Agreement Form—Stipulated Sum for Furniture, Furnishings, and Equipment,* with A271: *General Conditions of the Contract for Furniture, Furnishings, and Equipment* for purchase of the furniture; and A101: *Owner-Contractor Agreement Form—Stipulated Sum,* with A201: *General Conditions of the Contract for Construction* for construction work

47. Which of these organizations publish standards that might be referred to in an interior door specification? (Choose the four that apply.)

    A. UL
    B. AWI
    C. TCNA
    D. FSC
    E. CSI
    F. WDMA

48. Which of the following is NOT a part of the contract documents?

    A. an addendum
    B. bidding documents
    C. general conditions of the contract for construction
    D. change orders

49. Which of the following would NOT be considered a part of the net assignable area of a building?

    A. a classroom
    B. a lobby
    C. a janitor's closet
    D. a storage room

50. Which of the following statements about life-cycle cost analysis is FALSE?

    A. Higher up-front costs often lead to lower operational costs.
    B. It is economical to complete a life-cycle cost analysis if two items have similar installation costs but differing operational costs or projected lifespans.
    C. Life-cycle cost analysis evaluates all costs based upon their present value.
    D. Costs presented in the analysis are the only factors that should be considered when making a decision about a material or system.

PROFESSIONAL PUBLICATIONS, INC.

51.   A contractor submits the following bid form.

> Tussey Mountain Construction
> 6734 Raystown Road
> Saxton, Pennsylvania
>
> *BASE BID: The undersigned, having inspected the construction site and familiarized him/herself with all conditions likely to be encountered affecting the cost and schedule of work, and having examined all of the Contract Documents, hereby proposes to furnish all labor, materials, tools, equipment, and services required to perform all of the work in strict accordance with the Contract Documents for the Base Bid Sum of:*
>
> Seven hundred fifty-six thousand, four hundred fifty-two dollars and 0/100 dollars
> $765,452.00
>
> *and if this proposal is accepted, will execute a formal contract to this effect.*

How should the architect interpret this bid?

- A.   The bid is $765,452.
- B.   The bid is $756,452.
- C.   The bid is invalid and must be discarded.
- D.   The architect should call the bidder and ask him what amount was intended.

52.   When were the General Conditions first published?

- A.   1888
- B.   1911
- C.   1915
- D.   1916

53.   Which of the following is the best way to modify a standard AIA document?

- A.   Retype the document, incorporating all of the changes.
- B.   Attach supplementary conditions or amendments.
- C.   Strike out portions of the contract by hand or insert handwritten additions.
- D.   Have an attorney draft a new contract.

54.   "Claims-made" professional liability insurance policies

- A.   base the cost of the insurance policy on the number of claims made against it
- B.   require the policy to be in effect at the time a claim is made, not merely at the time services were rendered
- C.   will cover a claim made against a retired partner if the policy was in effect at the time the incident that caused the claim occurred, but is no longer held by the firm
- D.   are canceled if more than one claim is made against it in a specified period of time

55.   An analysis of the financial feasibility of a potential project is called a

- A.   project budget
- B.   feasibility study
- C.   program
- D.   pro forma

56.   Which type of construction fee structure would encourage a contractor to be most efficient?

- A.   cost-plus with a fixed, lump-sum fee for overhead and profit
- B.   cost-plus with the fee for overhead and profit based upon a percentage of construction cost
- C.   stipulated sum
- D.   unit price

57.   A contractor submits a list of proposed subcontractors to the owner and architect for construction of a small office building. The architect reviews it and notes that the proposed plumbing subcontractor is a company with a history of poor workmanship; one of the architect's clients on a previous project spent thousands of dollars to correct the plumber's errors. The architect expresses his concerns to the owner, who agrees that he would prefer not to have this subcontractor as a part of the project. If the owner-contractor agreement references the General Conditions (AIA Document A201), what can the owner and architect do?

A. nothing, as the selection of subcontractors is entirely within the purview of the general contractor and the list of subcontractors is submitted to the architect and owner for information only

B. submit to the contractor the name and contact information for a plumbing subcontractor the owner would prefer to use for the project and require the contractor to hire that firm

C. require the general contractor to use a different plumbing subcontractor with no adjustment to the contract sum

D. require the general contractor to use a different plumbing subcontractor, with the understanding that the contract sum or contract time may be adjusted to reflect the new subcontractor's proposed price and/or schedule

58. Many AIA documents require parties to the agreements to submit their disputes to arbitration. Which of the following statements regarding arbitration is FALSE?

A. Arbitration is generally less expensive than litigation.

B. If the agreement states that arbitration is binding, either party may appeal the findings.

C. If two parties sign a contract agreeing to submit disputes to arbitration, they must do so.

D. Both parties are given an opportunity to object to potential arbitrators.

59. Identify the following material symbols.

I.

II.

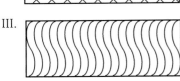

III.

IV.

A. I–terrazzo, II–ceramic tile, III–concrete block, IV–rigid insulation

B. I–ceramic tile, II–concrete block, III–rigid insulation, IV–terrazzo

C. I–concrete block, II–terrazzo, III–rigid insulation, IV–ceramic tile

D. I–rigid insulation, II–concrete block, III–ceramic tile, IV–terrazzo

60. Which of the following is least likely to be found in a local zoning ordinance?

A. minimum setbacks from property lines

B. maximum building height

C. maximum floor area ratio

D. types of materials that may be used for construction

61. When is the ideal time to "value engineer" a project?

A. in the initial planning stages

B. at the end of the design development phase

C. after the construction documents have been completed

D. after bids are received and they all exceed the owner's budget

62. According to the U.S. National CAD Standard system of organizing construction documents, what type of drawings would one expect to find on sheet A-302?

A. wall sections

B. fourth-floor plan

C. exterior elevations

D. reflected ceiling plans

63. Five general contractors are invited to bid on a small office renovation project. The drawings are mailed to the bidders at the beginning of June, with bids due on July 2. The documents state that bidders are to list a unit price per square yard for providing and installing carpet. In the meantime, the owner decides to choose and order carpet through a local flooring distributor and provide it to the contractor to install. The architect issues an addendum to this effect on June 22, requesting that bidders delete the unit price and include installation of the carpet in their bids. Upon receipt of the addendum, one of the prospective bidders calls the architect and says that he has already delivered his bid to the owner's office, as stated in the instructions to bidders. How should the architect respond?

A. Ask the contractor the amount he wishes to add to or deduct from the price and adjust the bid after the bid opening.

B. Tell the contractor to retrieve the bid from the owner, correct it to reflect receipt of the addendum and the revised price, and resubmit it to the owner.

C. Tell the contractor to submit another bid.

D. Explain that the bid will not be considered valid without acknowledgement of receipt of the addendum.

64. When an architect makes an impartial interpretation of the contract documents during construction administration, in accordance with the general conditions, in what capacity is he considered to be acting?

A. arbitratory
B. quasi-judicial
C. mediative
D. professional

65. An architect is visiting a project site on a rainy afternoon to observe the progress of work and certify a pay application. While photographing the site, she witnesses a construction worker fall from scaffolding after slipping on a wet board. The worker is obviously injured and appears to be unconscious. What should the architect do?

A. Call 911, notify the superintendent immediately, and fully document the accident with a written report and photographs.

B. Report the incident to the superintendent immediately.

C. Conduct an investigation.

D. Do nothing; construction safety is the responsibility of the contractor.

66. Which of the following statements would be most acceptable for an architect to certify?

A. "The architect certifies to the owner that, in the architect's professional opinion, the contractor has spent the amount indicated and the contractor is entitled to payment in the amount certified."

B. "The architect certifies to the owner that, to the best of the architect's knowledge, information, and belief, the work has progressed to the point indicated, the quality of the work is in accordance with the contract documents, and the contractor is entitled to payment in the amount certified."

C. "The architect certifies that the contract documents comply with all applicable codes, standards, and regulations."

D. "Based on the architect's observations and other information available to the architect, the contractor has complied with the International Building Code throughout the course of construction."

67. Four years ago, an architecture firm completed the design of a new high school. Construction was completed two years later. A year and a half after final completion, the district superintendent calls the architect and explains that there is a leak in the roof of the chemistry classroom. The architect informs the contractor and then schedules a meeting at the site to investigate the situation. Upon investigation, it is found that the work is constructed in compliance with the requirements of the contract documents, but that one of the roofing membranes became brittle when exposed to the sun and has begun to crack. Who is responsible for correcting the problem?

A. the roofing manufacturer
B. the school district
C. the contractor
D. there is not enough information given to answer the question

68. Which of the following would NOT be considered a reimbursable expense and could NOT be charged to the owner by the architect, assuming that their agreement is based upon AIA Document B141?

  A. plan review fees paid to the local code enforcement office

  B. overtime work

  C. a $1 million increase to the architect's liability coverage, requested by the owner

  D. upgrading from an earlier version of CAD software to the most current release

69. Indirect liability imposed on a party resulting from the acts or omissions of another person for whom the party is responsible is known as

  A. transferred liability

  B. vicarious liability

  C. consultant liability

  D. limited liability

70. The shaded area in the following map of Williamsburg, Virginia, represents the areas in which all proposed additions, renovations, and new construction must be reviewed by the city's Architectural Review Board. Which type of zoning strategy is this is an example of?

  A. a planned unit development

  B. cluster zoning

  C. overlay zoning

  D. inclusionary zoning

71. Which of the following is a common exclusion of an all-risk insurance policy?

  A. fire damage

  B. vandalism

  C. acts of war

  D. boiler explosion

72. The majority of fire deaths occur in

  A. dormitories

  B. single-family residences

  C. high-rise office buildings

  D. nightclubs

73. Which of these statements regarding building officials is FALSE?

  A. If a building should collapse, the building official could be held personally liable for failing to properly inspect the structure whether or not he or she acted in good faith.

  B. A building official has the right to enter any building at a reasonable time if he believes that the building is not in compliance with the code or is unsafe.

  C. The interpretation of the building official having jurisdiction becomes the final decision.

  D. A user cannot occupy a property until the building official has completed a final inspection and issued a certificate of occupancy.

74. Which of the following factors would have the greatest impact to reduce the effect of inclement weather on construction time?

  A. the use of prefabricated elements

  B. the use of designs that contribute to improved sequencing

  C. the use of union labor

  D. beginning construction in the spring

75.   The contractor must submit the application for payment to the architect _____ days in advance of the payment date. (Fill in the blank.)

76.   The owners of a residential project plan to shop for and purchase all the kitchen appliances in their new home. They want the contractor to be responsible for coordinating the electricity, gas, and plumbing, and for installing the equipment. How should these items be noted on the drawings?

    A.   "N.I.C."
    B.   "owner furnished-contractor installed"
    C.   "cash allowance"
    D.   by name, as "range," "refrigerator," and so on

77.   The general, supplementary, and special conditions do NOT

    A.   establish duties of the owner and contractor
    B.   define legal rights of the parties
    C.   establish duties of the architect
    D.   establish administrative procedures for the project

78.   Which of the following materials would have the smallest dimensional tolerances?

    A.   precast concrete tees
    B.   2×4 wood framing at a window opening
    C.   steel beams
    D.   wood paneling

79.   Which of these statements regarding scheduling is FALSE?

    A.   Each item listed on the critical path must be completed by the target date or the project completion date will be affected.
    B.   From the contractor's perspective, it is best if the duration of each activity is less than the period between progress payments.
    C.   Sequencing is generally depicted on a bar chart.
    D.   Float is a property of activities that can be started or finished within a prescribed time range and not affect the project completion date.

80.   During a hotel construction project in the Outer Banks of North Carolina, a hurricane slams into the coast, leveling a building that was framed one week prior. Which type of clause permits the contractor to request a change to the contract time or contract sum due to the damage?

    A.   indemnification
    B.   joinder
    C.   force majeure
    D.   named peril

81.   The indemnification provision in AIA Document A201 indemnifies

I.   the contractor
II.   the owner
III.   the architect
IV.   the subcontractor

    A.   II only
    B.   I and IV only
    C.   II and III only
    D.   I, II, and III only

82.   AIA Document B141 forms the legal relationship between the owner and the architect. Article 1.1, Initial Information, defines the project parameters. Which of the following pieces of information is NOT requested of the owner at the beginning of a project?

    A.   a physical description of the proposed site
    B.   certification from the owner's lender or financiers that adequate funds are available to pay for design and construction of the proposed project
    C.   a proposed schedule, including any special requirements such as "fast-tracking"
    D.   a proposed procurement and delivery method, such as a negotiated contract, competitive bidding, or employment of a construction manager

83.   A potential client calls a small architecture firm and explains that he has a set of house plans purchased from a shelter magazine. He submitted the drawings to the local township for a building permit, but was denied because the drawings did not include sufficient information, such as a foundation plan, and did not comply with local guidelines for insulation requirements. He asks if the firm can use the CAD files that he purchased along with the prints to produce drawings that he can submit for a building permit. How should the architect respond?

A.   Advise him to contact the company that sold him the drawings and request that they revise them to include sufficient information to obtain the building permit.

B.   Politely decline the job, explaining that it is a violation of the NCARB Rules of Conduct and of copyright to modify another designer's work.

C.   Accept the job, contingent upon receiving proper permission from the original author of the drawings.

D.   Any of the above answers are acceptable; each firm must evaluate these types of projects on a case-by-case basis.

84.   Which of the following would NOT be an appropriate reason to issue architect's supplemental instructions (AIA Document G710)?

A.   The owner and architect decide to delete under-cabinet lighting from all of the kitchens in an apartment project.

B.   The architect changes the location of a few lighting fixtures in a suspended grid ceiling to better illuminate workstations shown on the interior designer's modular furniture plan.

C.   In the course of answering a question from the contractor, the architect notices a discrepancy between the plan and section and prepares a sketch to clarify the drawings.

D.   The architect revises the color schedule based on the manufacturers' products the contractor intends to install.

85.   Which of the following statements is true?

A.   "Clerk of the works" is another term for the architect's project representative.

B.   If a contractor discovers an error in the contract documents, the architect is required to absorb the cost of correcting the drawings and pay for the cost of construction related to the error.

C.   A construction change directive must be signed by the contractor to be valid.

D.   The contractor is responsible for notifying the surety of any change orders issued during a project.

86.   An architect and the developer of a small office complex are preparing the project manual for a new project. The architect asks the owner for information regarding insurance requirements for this project. The owner, in turn, asks the architect what types of coverage and how much coverage he will need for the project. What is the most appropriate way for the architect to respond?

I.   Provide the owner with a copy of AIA Document G612, *Owner's Instructions Regarding the Construction Contract, Insurance and Bonds, and Bidding*.

II.   Give the owner some ballpark numbers based on previous projects.

III. Advise the owner to consult with his insurance agent.

IV.   Help the owner to determine reasonable amounts.

A.   I and II
B.   I and III
C.   I and IV
D.   II and IV

87.   Under an agreement referencing AIA Document A201, who is required to file a certificate of insurance prior to commencement of work?

A.   the owner
B.   the contractor
C.   the architect
D.   the subcontractor

88.   During which phase of a project are project requirements defined, early sketches developed, and preliminary cost estimates completed?

A.   programming
B.   schematic design
C.   design development
D.   construction documents

89.   The joinder provisions in AIA Documents A201 and B141

    A.   permit issues involving the owner, contractor, and architect to be resolved in one arbitration

    B.   prohibit parties other than those joined by the contract from being included in arbitration under the agreement

    C.   allow two parties to "team up" against the other to share legal expenses

    D.   prohibit a subcontractor from being called as a witness against the contractor

90.   A renovation project at a large classroom building on a college campus is scheduled to take place in two phases during the next summer and the winter break, when classes are not in session. All windows in the building are to be replaced, and the window manufacturer advises the college to purchase all the windows at one time to take advantage of considerable savings. The college facilities staff thinks this is a good idea but does not have room to store the windows on campus, so the college requests that the contractor purchase and store the windows until they are needed. The contractor submits the first pay application, which includes a request for payment for 80% of the windows line item on the schedule of values. What is the minimum that the architect should do prior to certifying the pay application?

I.   Request copies of bills of sale and insurance for the windows.

II.   Visit the location where the windows are stored.

III.   Submit documentation to the owner's attorney for evaluation prior to certifying the pay application.

IV.   Request written approval from the owner.

    A.   I only

    B.   I and II only

    C.   II and IV only

    D.   I, II, III, and IV

91.   Which of the following terms should NOT be used by an architect to describe services offered?

I.   supervision of construction

II.   as-built drawings of a completed project or existing building

III.   certification of applications for payment

IV.   periodic site visits during construction, including attendance at a weekly job conference

    A.   I only

    B.   I and II only

    C.   II and III only

    D.   I, II, and IV only

92.   In life-cycle cost analysis, costs incurred prior to the baseline date are referred to as

    A.   uniform costs

    B.   break-even costs

    C.   sunk costs

    D.   sensitive costs

93.   Which of these statements about mechanics' liens is true?

    A.   A mechanic's lien gives a contractor, subcontractor, or supplier clear title to an owner's property.

    B.   Liens are permitted on publicly owned projects.

    C.   A lien applies to all of the owner's assets.

    D.   A contractor must provide evidence that a project is free of liens before receiving payment.

94.   AIA Document C141, *Standard Form of Agreement Between Architect and Consultant*, does NOT require the consultant to

    A.   provide construction administration services

    B.   assist with evaluating bids

    C.   prepare cost estimates

    D.   carry liability insurance

95.   An architectural firm should retain project records

    A.   for five years after substantial completion

    B.   until the statute of repose period has ended

    C.   until the statute of limitations period has ended

    D.   indefinitely

96.   In AIA Document A101, Article 3, the date of commencement for a small remodeling project is March 15. The contractor is required to achieve substantial completion in 60 days. When is the target date for substantial completion?

    A.   May 13

    B.   May 15

    C.   June 6

    D.   June 8

97. A continuous vertical section of a brick wall is called a

    A. course

    B. face

    C. veneer

    D. wythe

98. According to AIA Document B141, the architect must revise the construction cost estimate if bidding does not commence within

    A. 90 days after the start of the project

    B. 90 days after completion of the preliminary cost estimate

    C. 90 days after the architect submits the construction documents to the owner

    D. none of the above; bidding dates have no effect on the construction cost estimate

99. Which of the following is NOT a characteristic of the design-build approach to project delivery, as compared to the design-award-build model?

    A. The owner has more control over the quality of the materials and the types of construction methods used to build the project.

    B. The owner has more information about the cost of the project available at an earlier phase in the project.

    C. The combined design and construction time is generally less.

    D. The owner must approach the project with a clearly defined program or set of performance requirements.

100. An architect suspects that blocking has been installed in the wrong location and asks that a portion of the work be uncovered. When the drywall is removed, the blocking is found to be in the correct location. Who is responsible for paying for the removal and replacement of the portion of the wall?

    A. the architect

    B. the owner

    C. the contractor

    D. the architect and owner should split the cost

PRACTICE EXAM: VIGNETTE

BUILDING SECTION

Directions

Draw a schematic building section corresponding to the section cut line shown on the following plans for a two-story building. Include the grade line, exterior walls, foundation, slab on grade, interior bearing walls, partitions, finished ceilings, structural elements, and HVAC ducts. Draw only the elements that are cut by the cut line, and draw joists in elevation immediately adjacent to the cut line. The section must accurately reflect the dimensions and spatial relations given in the program and on the plans. Vertical spacing not explicitly stated in the program must be accurately interpreted and indicated on the section.

Program

The structural system consists of top-chord bearing steel joists on masonry bearing walls with continuous concrete spread footings and a 6 in (152) concrete slab on grade.

1. The roof and all ceilings are flat with a 4 in (100) concrete slab on the joists.

2. Nonbearing corridor and library walls have a 1-hour (minimum) fire-resistance rating.

3. Exterior and bearing walls have a 2-hour fire rating.

4. The ceiling height of the library is 16 ft 0 in (5030). For other spaces this is 8 ft 6 in (2590).

5. Ceilings are nonrated and used as return air plenums.

6. Assume fire and smoke dampers and transfer grilles are provided as needed.

7. The space between each ceiling and floor or roof slab must be held to the minimum needed to accommodate light fixtures and the mechanical and structural components shown on the plans.

8. All ducts are placed below the joists.

9. Provide 12 in (300) of clearance between the bottoms of the ducts and the finished ceiling to accommodate light fixtures.

10. The frost depth is 3 ft 0 in (915) below grade.

11. Parapets must extend 2 ft 6 in (760) above the surface of decks at roof edges and at changes in the roof deck elevation.

12. The site is level.

13. Footings are to be 1 ft by 3 ft (305 by 914).

Tips

- Study each floor plan by turning layers on and off.
- It may be useful to start by laying out a rough drawing and adjusting individual elements later.
- Use the *move group* tool to relocate an entire joist run. Use the *move, adjust* tool to change the location of the joists within the joist run.
- Zoom in frequently to make fine adjustments.
- If one element of two overlapping elements cannot be selected, keep clicking without moving the mouse until the desired element is highlighted.

Warnings

- A grade line *must* be drawn for the section to be graded.

Tools

Useful tools include the following.

- layers to turn elements on and off in order to view the base drawings more clearly
- *zoom* tool to draw and adjust individual elements
- *sketch line* tool for establishing heights and clearances
- full-screen cursor to help align elements

Target Time: 1 hour

59

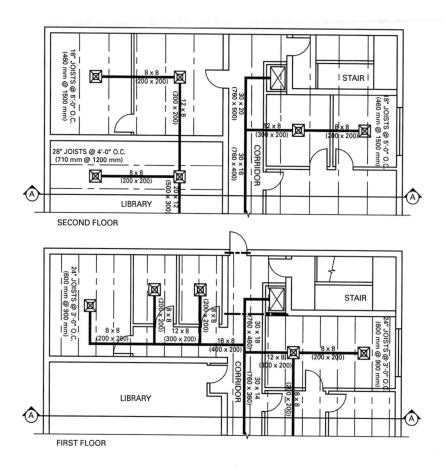

SECOND FLOOR

FIRST FLOOR

Scale: 1/16" = 1'-0"
(1:200 metric)

BUILDING SECTION

PRACTICE EXAM: MULTIPLE CHOICE SOLUTIONS

1. C
2. C
3. C
4. B, D
5. D
6. A
7. D
8. A
9. C
10. B
11. C
12. A
13. B
14. A
15. B
16. A
17. B
18. B
19. B
20. D
21. B
22. B
23. B
24. C
25. A

26. B
27. __3__
28. D
29. C
30. C
31. D
32. A, B, C, D
33. A
34. D
35. D
36. A
37. A, B, C, F
38. D
39. D
40. D
41. C
42. C
43. B
44. C
45. C
46. D
47. A, B, D, F
48. B
49. B
50. D

51. B
52. B
53. B
54. B
55. D
56. A
57. D
58. B
59. D
60. D
61. A
62. A
63. B
64. B
65. A
66. B
67. D
68. D
69. B
70. C
71. C
72. B
73. A
74. A
75. __10 days__

76. (A) ● (C) (D)   90. (A) ● (C) (D)
77. (A) (B) (C) ●   91. (A) ● (C) (D)
78. (A) (B) (C) ●   92. (A) (B) ● (D)
79. (A) (B) ● (D)   93. (A) (B) (C) ●
80. (A) (B) ● (D)   94. (A) (B) (C) ●
81. (A) (B) ● (D)   95. (A) ● (C) (D)
82. (A) ● (C) (D)   96. ● (B) (C) (D)
83. (A) (B) (C) ●   97. (A) (B) (C) ●
84. ● (B) (C) (D)   98. (A) (B) ● (D)
85. (A) (B) (C) ●   99. ● (B) (C) (D)
86. (A) ● (C) (D)   100. (A) ● (C) (D)
87. (A) ● (C) (D)
88. (A) ● (C) (D)
89. (A) ● (C) (D)

1. The answer is C.

The AIA Contract Documents are organized by letter series. Each letter series classifies documents according to the end users. They are grouped as follows.

A-series   owner-contractor documents

B-series   owner-architect documents

C-series   architect-consultant documents

D-series   architect-industry documents

G-series   architect's office and project management forms

The documents are then further divided into "families" depending on the type of project for which they are most appropriate, such as interiors, small projects, or projects involving a construction manager. Documents within a family can come from a variety of letter series.

2. The answer is C.

According to the NCARB Rules of Conduct, an architect may sign and seal technical submissions if they are

- prepared by the architect

- prepared by persons under the architect's "responsible control," which means that the architect has as much professional knowledge of the work done by the employee as if he or she had completed it personally

- prepared by another registered architect in that jurisdiction if the architect has reviewed the submission and incorporated the other architect's work into his or her own submission or coordinated its preparation

- prepared by another NCARB-certified architect who is registered in the United States, if the technical submissions have been reviewed by the architect and incorporated into his work or if they are prototypical building documents

Documents and work not required by law to be prepared by an architect may be signed and sealed by another architect if they are thoroughly reviewed and integrated with the architect's submission.

Special provisions exist when work is done by a person who is under the architect's responsible control but is not regularly employed in the architect's office. Such a case is described in this question. The temporary employee is working under the direction and supervision of the architect to provide drafting services necessary to prepare drawings. The drafter is presumably working from sketches and design information prepared by the architect, and the drafter's work will be thoroughly reviewed and incorporated into the construction documents by the architect of record. The architect remains responsible for the design and the accuracy of the technical submission. This is permissible according to the NCARB Rules of Conduct; however, it is necessary for the architect of record or the firm to retain documentation of the drafter's involvement with the project and the architect's supervision of that work for five years.

The NCARB Rules of Conduct were developed to serve as recommendations for state licensing boards, but each state is responsible for developing its own standards of professional conduct. These requirements may differ from state to state or from NCARB's Rules of Conduct. However, for the ARE, candidates should be familiar with NCARB's standards. A copy of these standards may be downloaded from NCARB's website at www.ncarb.org.

3. The answer is C.

AIA Document A201 addresses issues of insurance and bonds in Article 11. Subparagraph 11.3.1 discusses *project management protective liability* insurance, which offers coverage for vicarious liability claims related to a project against the owner, contractor, and architect. An owner is not required to carry project management protective liability insurance, but may require a contractor to carry it. If the owner requires the contractor to carry this insurance, the owner must reimburse the contractor for its cost.

The owner is required to purchase all of the other types of insurance. *All-risk* property insurance, which includes everything but specifically named risks, is required by Article 11.4.1. *Boiler and machinery* insurance is required by Subparagraph 11.4.2 and covers only those items until final acceptance of the work. Subparagraph 11.2.1 requires the owner to carry *liability* insurance throughout the project.

Architects are not qualified to give clients advice regarding insurance coverage. Architects can use AIA Document G612, *Owner's Instructions Regarding the Construction Contract, Insurance and Bonds, and Bidding*, to gather information about their client's insurance requirements for the purposes of preparing the contract documents. Owners should be advised to consult with an attorney or insurance agent if they have questions about insurance recommendations for the project.

4. The answer is B, D, and E.

Both *corporations* and *limited-liability companies* limit individual liability to the amount invested. A *limited-liability partnership*, like a limited-liability company, also limits liability to a person's investment.

A traditional *partnership* exposes each partner to liability for the actions of the other partners. The partners' personal assets can be seized to pay judgments against the firm.

A *sole proprietor* is personally liable for everything, and his or her personal resources can be taken in the event of a claim.

Disadvantaged business enterprises, like minority- or women-owned business enterprises, are small businesses certified by some states in order to encourage more participation from these groups in government-funded projects.

5. The answer is D.

The *contract documents*, which are comprised of the agreement, conditions of the contract, drawings, specifications, addenda, and any other documents listed in the agreement, *are* the contract between the owner and the contractor according to AIA Document A201, Subparagraph 1.1.2. This article goes on to explain that this contract is only between these two parties and that no other project participant is contractually obligated to another by this agreement.

6. The answer is A.

Retainage is a percentage of the contract sum held back from applications for payment, usually around 10%. The money is paid to the contractor when the project has been completed satisfactorily; in the meantime, the retainage gives the owner leverage to ensure that the work is completed on time and in accordance with the construction documents. Retainage also helps to protect the owner against lien claims by ensuring that the owner has funds available to pay for materials or labor should the contractor fail to pay for them. Before retainage is released or decreased, the surety company that provided the contractor's performance bond should give written consent to the payment.

7. The answer is D.

To prove negligence, four elements must be present.

- *duty*: one entity is legally obligated to another to provide something

- *breach*: one entity did not provide what they were legally obligated to provide

- *cause*: because one entity did not provide what they were obligated to provide, the other entity has suffered harm

- *damage*: there must be actual harm caused as a result of the breach

Negligence claims can be brought about from errors of omission on the part of the architect.

8. The answer is A.

A local code official would be authorized to enforce all of the codes or standards listed except the Americans with Disabilities Act guidelines. The ADA is civil rights legislation that gives building users the right to sue the owner of a building if they are denied access to a facility because the building is not accessible. The other three choices are model codes or standards that, when adopted by a community government, become the building code. Depending on the jurisdiction, the code official could enforce ANSI A117.1 or the Americans with Disabilities Act Accessibility Guidelines (ADAAG), either of which can be adopted to define the standards for accessibility.

9. The answer is C.

The architect should return the samples to the subcontractor without reviewing them. The subcontractor should first submit them to the contractor for review for compliance with the construction documents, in accordance with AIA Document A201, Subparagraph 3.12.5. The contractor may them submit them to the architect for review and selections.

10. The answer is B.

Subparagraph 2.6.2.5 of AIA Document B141 gives the architect the authority to reject work that is not in compliance with the construction documents. To determine whether work is in compliance, the architect has the authority to require third-party testing or sampling. Subparagraph 4.2.6 of AIA Document A201 notifies the contractor of this authority.

Only the owner has the authority to stop work (AIA Document A201, Subparagraph 2.3.1), order changes that affect the cost or duration of the project through a change order or construction change directive (AIA Document A201, Subparagraphs 7.2.1 and 7.3.1), or accept nonconforming work (AIA Document A201, Subparagraph 12.3.1).

The architect can order minor changes that do not affect the contract sum or time (AIA Document A201, Subparagraph 7.4.1, and AIA Document B141, Subparagraph 2.6.5.1), but it is generally advisable to inform the owner as soon as practicable and obtain written agreement with the change.

11.   The answer is C.

The supplementary conditions should include information about basic legal rights and responsibilities that may vary from one project to another. This includes insurance, indemnification, liquidated damages, legal requirements of the jurisdiction that may differ from the standard language in the general conditions, and fiduciary obligations. Instructions for preparing the supplementary conditions are available in AIA Document A511, *Guide for Supplementary Conditions*. The owner and the owner's legal and/or insurance counsel are responsible for preparing these modifications, not the architect.

Administrative procedures are properly addressed in the specifications in Division 01, General Requirements.

12.   The answer is A.

Construction drawings are generally organized in the following sequence.

- title sheet and identifying information
- civil or site drawings
- architectural drawings
- structural drawings (on some projects, structural drawings are placed before architectural drawings)
- plumbing, mechanical, and electrical drawings (order may vary by office)
- other consultants' drawings

Within the category of architectural drawings, the sheets are generally placed in the following order.

- demolition plans (if applicable)
- floor plans
- reflected ceiling plans
- roof plans
- elevations: exterior and interior
- sections: building sections and wall sections
- details: exterior and interior
- schedules

13.   The answer is B.

The architect's specification defines the product desired, but the inclusion of the phrase "or approved equal" allows the contractor to propose a different type of tile that may be less expensive or easier to obtain within the project time frame. The contractor must submit any requests for substitutions prior to the bid. The responsibility for researching alternative products falls to the contractor, who must submit technical data with his request. Enough time must be allowed prior to the bid for the architect to review the substitution and issue an addendum notifying all potential bidders of the change.

14.   The answer is A.

MasterFormat™, developed by the Construction Specifications Institute (CSI), is a system of organizing information related to construction projects. The old 16-division format was replaced in 2004 with a new system that is broken down into 50 divisions, to allow for the inclusion of new technologies and better organization of information for a variety of project types.

The 50 divisions are further classified into groups and subgroups. The two major groups are the Procurement and Contracting Requirements Group, Division 00, which contains bidding and contract information, and the Specifications Group, which consists of Divisions 01 through 49.

ARE candidates should be familiar with the General Requirements, Facility Construction, Facility Services, and Site and Infrastructure subgroups, and know that bidding and contract information is contained within Division 00.

A full list of MasterFormat 2004 Divisions can be found in PPI's *ARE Review Manual*.

15.   The answer is B.

Shop drawings, samples, and cut sheets are commonly included in contractors' submittals. Submittals are addressed in both AIA Document B141, Subparagraph 2.6.4, and AIA Document A201, Subparagraph 3.12. Administrative procedures regarding submittals should be defined in Division 00 of the specifications.

Submittals are prepared by or on behalf of the contractor specifically for the project and are submitted to the architect to explain the products the contractor intends to install. The contractor is responsible for verifying materials and dimensional information and for coordinating the information in the submittal with the project as a whole. The architect reviews the information for the purpose of confirming that the products are in accordance with the requirements of the construction documents and the design intent. If the submittal deals with a system or materials specified by a consultant, the architect should forward it to the appropriate consultant for their review, and upon return, review and stamp it. After review of any submittal, the architect should stamp the submittal and mark it "approved," "approved as corrected (or indicated)," "revise and resubmit," or "not approved" and return it to the contractor.

MSDSs, or Materials Safety Data Sheets, are prepared by any supplier of hazardous materials. This information is required by the Occupational Safety and Health Administration (OSHA) for any materials used in a workplace and must be kept current and accessible to employees during working hours. The documents include information on the physical properties of the chemicals, required protective equipment, appropriate responses to exposure, and health risks.

16.   The answer is A.

The contractor is technically responsible for the additional cost incurred because AIA Document A201, Subparagraph 1.5.2 explains that "execution of the Contract by the Contractor is a representation that the Contractor has visited the site, become generally familiar with local conditions under which the Work is to be performed, and correlated personal observations with requirements of the Contract Documents." However, that same document states in Subparagraph 2.2.3 that the "Contractor shall be entitled to rely on the accuracy of information furnished by the Owner."

AIA Document A201 includes a provision to address this sort of situation, where concealed conditions differ from those anticipated by the contract documents. Subparagraph 4.3.4 allows either party to submit a claim for concealed or unknown conditions within 21 days of discovery. This provision helps the owner and contractor to negotiate a fair resolution to the issue and protects the owner from bid prices that may be inflated to allow for the unknown conditions.

Unless it can be proven that the soils report was in error, the geotechnical engineer would probably not be held financially responsible for the additional work because it is nearly impossible to define all of the subsurface conditions on a site with absolute accuracy. The architect would not be responsible because he fulfilled his obligation to the client by making the owner aware of the prevalence of this condition locally and requesting that the owner arrange appropriate tests. It is also important to note that the soils test was not incorporated into the contract documents. The geotechnical engineer is hired by the owner, not the architect, so he is not acting as a consultant to the architect.

17.   The answer is B.

Architects do not issue occupancy permits; these permits are authorized by the code official in the project jurisdiction.

AIA Document B141, Subparagraph 2.6.6, deals with project completion. The architect must determine the date of substantial completion and final completion. The architect must also obtain from the contractor and forward to the owner any written warranties required by the contract documents, consent of the surety to release retainage and make the final payment, and releases or waivers of liens or bonds indemnifying the owner against liens. The architect must also prepare a final certificate for payment.

18.   The answer is B.

The contractor is required by AIA Document A201, Subparagraph 9.8.2, to prepare a punch list when the work is substantially complete. A *punch list* is a written summary of items that need to be repaired or corrected before final payment. *Substantial completion* is the point at which the project is complete enough for the owner to use it for its intended purpose. This is a critical point in the course of construction because it marks the date upon which the owner takes responsibility for insurance and utilities, and warranty periods for equipment begin.

The punch list is submitted to the architect, who is then responsible for completing an *inspection* of the project to determine whether the contractor's assessment is correct and the project is substantially complete. This is a more in-depth look at the project than the architect's earlier *observations*. The architect must verify that the contractor has complied with the requirements of the contract documents, and to do this, the architect may request assistance from consultants to verify the portions of the work that they designed.

If the architect agrees that substantial completion has been attained, a certificate of substantial completion is issued, which allows the owner to occupy and use the project and assume the responsibilities mentioned previously. The contractor then has a specified period of time to remedy items on the punch list before the architect returns for a final completion inspection.

19.   The answer is B.

There are three questions an architect must answer at the beginning of a project to determine the permitted size and layout of a building. The questions must be answered simultaneously, and the answers to each question are often dependent on the answers to the others (for example, fully sprinklered buildings can often be larger and of a less fire-resistive type of construction than buildings for similar uses that do not include a sprinkler system). The questions are as follows.

- *What is the occupancy of this building?* The occupancy is determined according to the owner's program, which defines the size and use of the spaces within the building. A building can be comprised of many different types of occupancies, which must be separated with appropriately fire-rated walls or partitions. The 2006 International Building Code lists the following occupancy classifications.

A	assembly
B	business
E	educational
F	factory and industrial
H	high hazard
I	institutional
M	mercantile
R	residential
S	storage
U	utility and miscellaneous

- *What type of fire-suppression system will be required?* Basically, this question ascertains whether or not the building will be sprinklered.

- *What type of construction will be used?* The 2006 International Building Code lists the following construction types.

types I and II	noncombustible materials
type III	exterior walls noncombustible, interior elements are of any materials complying with the code
type IV	heavy-timber construction
type V	exterior and interior elements are of any materials complying with the code

When the architect has determined the answers to these three questions, the information may be applied to the tables in the code to determine required means of egress, fire-separation requirements, and other code requirements that will govern design and materials selection.

20. The answer is D.

Although it is commonly believed that the specifications take precedence when there is a conflict between drawings and specs, AIA Document A201 clearly states that this is not the case. No order of precedence governs the interpretation of the contract documents; rather, they "are complementary, and what is required by one shall be as binding as if required by all." Subparagraph 1.2.1 goes on to state that the contractor is required to provide what is "reasonably inferable" from the contract documents.

If a conflict arises between two parts of the contract documents, the contractor should bring it to the architect's attention and ask for an interpretation. AIA Document A201, Subparagraph 4.2.11, gives the architect the responsibility to "interpret and decide matters concerning performance under, and requirements of, the Contract Documents on written request of either the Owner or Contractor." An interpretation of the contract documents that does not change the contract sum or contract time would be considered a minor modification to the work and would be within the architect's authority.

21. The answer is B.

Paragraph 10.3 of AIA Document A201 addresses the discovery of hazardous materials. The contractor was correct to stop work and immediately notify the owner of her suspicions, and the owner was correct to engage a testing agency to confirm that asbestos was present. The contractor has the right to an appropriate extension of the contract time and fair compensation for costs related to stopping and restarting the work. What is appropriate and fair is often negotiated between the owner and contractor, and the contract is modified by change order.

If the owner and contractor cannot agree, the contractor may assert a claim. While most claims are referred to the architect for an initial decision, claims dealing with hazardous materials always proceed directly to mediation and to arbitration if necessary.

22. The answer is B.

A physical or mental disability that impairs an architect's professional competence and a conflict of interest that is not properly disclosed to a client or employer are both considered by the NCARB Rules of Conduct to be violations that may bring about disciplinary action or revocation of an architect's license by a state licensing board. Each state's board has the responsibility of determining professional standards of conduct for architects, and these standards may differ from state to state or from NCARB's recommendations.

Items III and IV are not violations of the NCARB Rules of Conduct. In fact, Rule 3: Full Disclosure requires that architects who make public statements about projects or issues must reveal if they are working for one of the interested parties or if they have a financial stake in the issue. In Item III, the architect properly disclosed his affiliation with the resort developer. Item IV falls under NCARB Rule 5: Professional Conduct. Rule 5.3 prohibits improper gifts to clients or potential clients; however, gifts of nominal value, such as reasonable entertainment and hospitality, are excluded.

23.   The answer is B.

According to AIA Document A201, Subparagraph 3.10.2, the architect must approve the contractor's proposed schedule of submittals at the start of the project. This is to ensure that there will be a reasonable amount of time allowed for the architect to review the submittal, for the contractor to make corrections or revisions as necessary based upon the architect's review, and for the architect to approve the submittal without delaying the progress of the work.

Although the contractor must submit a construction schedule for the architect's review, the architect need not approve it. The contractor bears responsibility for coordinating and scheduling the work. Subparagraph 3.10.1 states that the schedule must show that the work will be completed within the time frame allotted and requires the contractor to revise the schedule as necessary to keep the architect and owner apprised of expected changes.

Subparagraph 3.11.1 requires the contractor to maintain a record copy of drawings, specifications, addenda, and other official project-related correspondence, including shop drawings and change orders. These are submitted to the architect for delivery to the owner at the end of the project. Record drawings are much more detailed and may be required of the contractor by the specifications, but AIA Document A201 does not include this requirement. (Record drawings are also often prepared by the architect as an additional service to the owner.)

The architect is responsible for reviewing only the submittals that are required by the contract documents according to Subparagraph 3.12.4. If additional submittals are forwarded to the architect, the architect may return them to the contractor without action.

24.   The answer is C.

The architect determines which submittals will be required while writing the project specifications. It is important to limit this requirement to items that warrant the architect's review. If the architect calls for unnecessary submittals, project administrative costs rise. If too few submittals are called for, there is a risk that the contractor may misinterpret the project requirements and order products that will not be acceptable. Submittals allow the architect to confirm that the design intent and requirements of the construction documents will be met by the products that the contractor proposes to include.

Submittals are generally required by the architect for natural materials (such as the wood paneling or granite countertops) where there can be a great deal of variation within a species or type. Items that are provided on a design-build basis, such as curtain walls, paneling or casework, and custom-built window assemblies, should require submittals. Shop drawings are commonly required for the steel framing system. The appearance and performance requirements of these components are defined in the construction documents, but the details of assembly may vary from one manufacturer to the next.

25.   The answer is A.

AIA Document A201, Article 9.5, addresses reasons that an architect may withhold a certificate for payment. The reasons include defective work not remedied, claims or probable claims against the project, failure of the contractor to pay subcontractors, damage to the owner or another contractor, evidence that the work will not be completed within the contract time, and persistent failure to carry out the work in accordance with the contract documents. The purpose of the architect's certification is to endeavor to protect the owner's interests in the project by not releasing payments until the contractor has properly completed the work.

Architects should always check over the math before certifying pay applications as this is a common source of error. Contractors often submit a rough draft, or *pencil copy*, for the architect's review before submitting the final pay application. This gives the architect a chance to point out errors or to raise questions with the contractor about work completed before the pay application is processed, which helps minimize delays.

26.   The answer is B.

Occupant load determines means-of-egress requirements: how many exits must be provided to evacuate a space in case of an emergency, how large the exits must be, and where they must be located. Design occupant load is tabulated under the 2006 International Building Code by using Table 1004.1.1.

standing space	5 net sq ft per occupant (0.4645 net m² per occupant)
concentrated (chairs only)	7 net sq ft per occupant (0.6503 net m² per occupant)
unconcentrated (tables and chairs)	15 net sq ft per occupant (1.3935 net m² per occupant)

The largest occupancy determines the egress requirements.

27. The answer is 3.

Unisex toilet rooms are required by the 2006 International Building Code where there are more than six separate-sex water closets required, and half of those provided (at least one) must be accessible. The fixtures provided in these rooms may count toward the total fixture requirement. Single-user toilet rooms are preferred by many for privacy and convenience. They are particularly useful in areas where there are lots of children, because they make it possible for a parent to accompany a child of the opposite sex to the restroom.

28. The answer is D.

AIA Document B141, Subparagraph 1.3.3, addresses changes in services and situations in which the architect is entitled to an adjustment to the schedule and compensation. The services defined in the agreement can be modified in writing and upon mutual agreement for circumstances beyond the architect's control. This prohibits the architect from benefiting from something that is his fault, such as the coordination error on the part of his consultants. The architect could hold the consultants responsible for their error, but could not receive compensation from the owner for additional time spent or expenses related to remedying the situation.

The second part of this subparagraph deals with circumstances where the owner delays the project because of indecision, changes to the project, or failure of performance on the part of consultants hired directly by the owner. All of these circumstances entitle the architect to an adjustment of deadlines and fees. Appearing at public hearings on the owner's behalf is also cited in this subparagraph, as well as the adoption of new codes or regulations midway through the project that require revisions to previously prepared documents.

29. The answer is C.

The cost of labor and materials is $22,250. The addition for overhead and profit would be 20%, for a total of 1.20 × $22,250, or $26,700.

The addition for coordination would be 5%, for a total of 1.05 × $26,700 = $28,035.

It would also be important to ensure that the owner receives proper credit for the deleted porcelain tile, including labor, materials, and overhead and profit; however, that information is not provided in the question.

30. The answer is C.

A *mock-up* is a full-scale preview of a building assembly. Mock-ups can be very expensive, so it is important to specify them only where they are truly necessary. Approved mock-ups can often be integrated into the work, making them more cost effective.

In this problem, the two best applications of mock-ups would be the apartment kitchens and the brick wall. In the case of the cabinetry, the mock-up would allow the architect and owner to see the kitchen in place and sign off on it before the contractor orders the materials for the other apartments. Modifications could be made relatively inexpensively based upon the mock-up, as opposed to waiting until all of the cabinets and countertops have been fabricated to make a change. A mock-up is also very useful where a contractor is charged with matching existing materials. A mock-up of the wall (or better yet, a few mock-ups representing different options) would allow the contractor to choose an appropriate brick color and style, mortar color, and tooling method, and to see how it will all work together before placing the order for the entire job.

There is no need to specify a mock-up for a CMU foundation wall, as this is a relatively standard detail. The carpet inlay would be an extremely expensive mock-up and could probably be more economically represented using a computer modeling program or a paper version of the design.

31. The answer is D.

Exit access travel distance is the maximum distance permitted from the most remote point within a space to the entrance of an exit. It is discussed in the 2006 International Building Code, Section 1016.

32.   The answer is A, B, C, and D.

The owner may choose any of the first four options listed, according to AIA Document B141, Subparagraph 2.1.7.5.

Abandoning the project would probably not be the best decision. The owner presumably has already invested a significant amount of money in design fees, and the design that has been developed is extremely close in price to the budget. A $10,000 difference on a $1.5 million job is less than 1% of the total construction cost. It would probably be wise for the owner to ask the architect to identify areas of potential savings and revise the drawings or specifications, if necessary. The owner would then have the option of rebidding the project or may be permitted to award the contract to the lowest qualified bidder, negotiate with the contractor, and modify the project through a change order to bring it in under the budget.

Rebidding the project generally would not result in much of a price difference unless there was reason to believe that market conditions would be very different at the time that the project goes out to bid the second time.

33.   The answer is A.

Subparagraph 11.3.3 prohibits the owner from requiring the contractor to include the owner, architect, or any other party on the contractor's liability insurance policy.

Each of the other statements is true. Choice B refers to Subparagraph 11.4.1.2; choice C refers to Subparagraph 11.3.1; and choice D refers to Subparagraph 11.4.1.3.

34.   The answer is D.

The International Building Code, instituted in 2000 to better standardize building codes across the United States, is a work in progress. The code is published by the International Code Council and is reviewed and revised every three years.

Anyone may propose a change to the building code; the procedure may be found on the ICC's website, www.iccsafe.org. The person making the proposal must complete forms identifying the text to be changed, the proposed modification, and a rationale for the change.

35.   The answer is D.

The low bidder is determined by the base bid plus any accepted bid alternates.

For ABC Construction,

$$\$244{,}150 + \$22{,}465 - \$6725 = \$259{,}890$$

For Sunny Day, Inc.,

$$\$265{,}430 + \$15{,}846 - \$5000 = \$276{,}276$$

For Grover and Sons,

$$\$270{,}000 + \$14{,}000 - \$2000 = \$282{,}000$$

For B&E General Contractors,

$$\$246{,}765 + \$18{,}768 - \$7500 = \$258{,}033$$

B&E General Contractors is the low bidder.

36.   The answer is A.

Accessory occupancies are discussed in Section 508.3.1 of the 2006 International Building Code. An *accessory occupancy* is a small area subsidiary to the primary occupancy of the building in which it is located.

37.   The answer is A, B, C, and F.

An *advertisement to bid* is published in a local newspaper to notify contractors of a project and give them the basic information necessary for them to obtain a set of bid documents for review. Public work is usually required to be advertised.

An advertisement to bid includes the following information.

- a name, location, and description of the project

- the name and address of the owner and architect

- instructions for obtaining a set of bidding documents and/or locations where bid documents may be viewed (such as plan rooms, the architect's office, etc.)

- the date, time, and location of the pre-bid conference, if scheduled

- the date, time, and location the bids are due

- the type and amount of bid bond required

- the date and time of the bid opening and whether or not the bids will be read publicly

- any other information that the owner or the owner's attorney feels should be included

38.   The answer is D.

Standard symbols on architectural drawings make it possible for architects, consultants, and contractors to communicate with a common, consistent language.

39.   The answer is D.

Wall sections are vertical "slices" of the exterior wall of a building that graphically depict how the building is to be built. They show vertical dimensions, materials, and relationships and how the pieces are intended to fit together.

40.   The answer is D.

The architect automatically has a copyright on the work as soon as it is produced in a tangible form. U.S. Copyright Office Circular 41: *Copyright Claims in Architectural Works* explains that the work "includes the overall form as well as the arrangement and composition of spaces and elements in the design but does not include individual standard features or design elements that are functionally required." The copyright for the architectural work itself is separate from the copyright on the technical drawings.

To enforce the copyright to the fullest extent, it is recommended, but not required, that the © symbol and date be placed on the drawings and a claim to copyright be registered with the U.S. Copyright Office.

For more information on copyright and architectural works, refer to Circular 41, available from the U.S. Copyright Office's website at www.copyright.gov.

41.   The answer is C.

A *common path of egress travel* is the part of the path of egress travel that occupants are required to move through before they reach a point where they have a choice to follow one of two distinct paths of travel to an exit.

The IBC uses specific terms to describe different parts of the path from a point inside a building to a safe point outside the building. The following definitions are from the 2006 edition.

- *area of refuge:* an area where people who are unable to use stairways can remain temporarily to await instructions or assistance during emergency evacuations

- *exit:* that portion of a means-of-egress system that is separated from other interior spaces of a building or structure by fire-resistance-rated construction and opening protectives as required to provide a protected path of egress travel between the exit access and the exit discharge

- *exit access:* that portion of a means-of-egress system that leads from any occupied portion of a building or structure to an exit

- *exit discharge:* that portion of a means-of-egress system between the termination of an exit and a public way

- *exit enclosure:* an exit component that is separated from all other interior spaces of a building or structure by fire-resistance-rated construction and opening protectives, and provides for a protected path of egress travel in a vertical or horizontal direction to the exit discharge or the public way

- *exit passageway:* an exit component that is separated from all other interior spaces of a building or structure by fire-resistance-rated construction and opening protectives, and provides for a protected path of egress travel in a horizontal direction to the exit discharge or the public way

- *egress court:* a court or yard that provides access to a public way for one or more exits

- *public way:* a street, alley, or other parcel of land open to the outside air leading to a street that has been deeded, dedicated, or otherwise appropriated for public use and has a clear width and height of not less than 10 ft (3048)

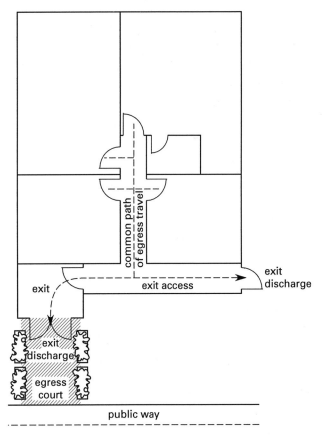

42.   The answer is C.

The owner's attorney should prepare the owner-contractor agreement, including the general conditions of the contract for construction and any supplementary conditions. Architects are not permitted to prepare contracts to which they are not a party; to do so would be the unauthorized practice of law and may even give rise to criminal liability. Preparing this agreement may require giving the owner legal or insurance advice, neither of which an architect is qualified to provide. Only the owner's legal counsel should prepare this document on the owner's behalf.

If the owner-contractor agreement proposed by the owner's attorney modifies the architect's responsibilities or risks in any way, the architect's insurance carrier and/or attorney should review it.

43.   The answer is B.

The *base bid with "approved equal"* language lists the desired product and states that an alternative product proposed by a contractor will be considered by the architect. This establishes a minimum level of quality based upon the characteristics of the specified product, but puts the responsibility on the contractor to find and submit an alternative product if he or she wishes. This type of specification will require the architect to evaluate the proposals during the bidding phase and issue addenda notifying all bidders of the decisions. When using a base bid with an "approved equal" type of specification, it is important to include a deadline for submission of proposed substitutions during the bidding phase to allow the architect enough time to research the products and issue notification to the bidders of the substitutions' acceptance or rejection.

A *proprietary* specification would not be the best choice in a situation where the owner and architect wish to encourage competitive bids. It specifies a particular product by brand name and allows no substitutions. This is the easiest type of specification for the architect to write, but puts all of the responsibility for choosing a material that is code-compliant and technically correct onto the architect.

A *base bid with alternates* specification is similar in format to the base bid with "approved equal" language specification. Both call for a specific product but allow substitution of other materials. However, an important difference between the two is that the base bid with alternates allows a contractor to substitute a product that he feels is equal, and does not require the architect's approval. The product he submits may not be comparable to the one defined in the specification but must be accepted due to the way the specification is written. This type of specification would not give the owner and architect control over the quality of the products used.

A *descriptive* specification defines the type of outcome desired but does not list specific products. It is the most difficult type of specification for an architect to write because it requires listing all of the criteria that a material or assembly must meet.

44.   The answer is C.

Instructions for installation would be found in Part III, Execution. This section describes how materials are to be prepared prior to installation, how substrates are to be prepared to accept the material, the methods for quality control, and requirements for cleaning and protecting the product after it is installed.

Part I, General, describes the submittals and warranties required for that product, project conditions, delivery, storage and handling requirements, and quality assurance requirements.

Part II, Products, includes information on the product, acceptable manufacturers, applicable standards and test methods, and technical requirements.

Division 01, General Requirements, includes requirements that apply to all specification sections. It explains the administrative procedures that will be used throughout the course of the project and gives the contractor instructions regarding issues such as temporary facilities and controls, submittals, items furnished by the owner, quality control, and final cleaning and protection of the work.

45.   The answer is C.

If a *penalty clause* (a charge to the contractor for not completing work by the agreed-upon time of substantial completion) is included in an agreement, a *bonus provision* (payment to the contractor if the work is completed before the deadline) must also be included. Penalty clauses are generally disfavored and when they appear alone they are almost always held unenforceable by courts. Thus, a penalty clause must be accompanied by a bonus clause, and even this does not guarantee that it will be enforceable. A better way to cover the owner for potential losses is to include a liquidated damages clause.

Liquidated damages are damages agreed upon in advance; they are based upon estimated costs that will be incurred by the owner if the contractor does not complete the work by the agreed-upon completion date and the owner cannot use the building at the anticipated time. For example, if the owner estimates that he will lose $1000 in profits each day that he cannot occupy his new dry cleaning business, liquidated damages may be assessed to cover this expense. His actual losses may be less or greater; liquidated damages represent a reasonable average.

Clauses requiring liquidated damages may also be accompanied by a bonus provision, but this is not required.

46. The answer is D.

The most appropriate choice of owner-contractor contracts for this project would be a combination of A101: *Owner-Contractor Agreement Form—Stipulated Sum* with A201: *General Conditions of the Contract for Construction* for the construction work, and A171: *Owner-Contractor Agreement Form—Stipulated Sum for Furniture, Furnishings, and Equipment* with A271: *General Conditions of the Contract for Furniture, Furnishings, and Equipment* for the purchase of the furniture. The contracts could both be with the same contractor, with two different contractors, or with a contractor and a furniture dealer.

Most AIA documents deal only with the provision of "traditional" architectural and construction services. The exceptions are the Interiors family, including A171 and A271, which were developed jointly by the AIA and ASID (American Society of Interior Designers). It is important to keep the design contract separate from the FF&E (fixtures, furnishings, and equipment) contract to preserve the architect's independence from monetary interest in the sale of the goods that the architect has specified. It is advisable to use the Interiors family documents in situations where the scope of the project is limited to FF&E because these forms reference the *Uniform Commercial Code*, which provides rules for commerce in the United States.

Documents in the Interiors family are not suitable for construction work such as the major tenant improvement described in this problem, or for projects with structural work or life safety systems. Therefore, portions of a project dealing with those issues should be covered under a separate agreement.

While the ARE focuses primarily on AIA Documents A101 and A201, it is a good idea to be familiar with the other AIA documents and situations in which they would be appropriate for use. One-paragraph summaries of each of the documents are available on the AIA website at www.aia.org/docs_synopses.

47. The answer is A, B, D, and F.

References to the Architectural Woodwork Institute's (AWI) *Quality Standards Illustrated* and the Forest Stewardship Council's (FSC) *Principles and Criteria* would commonly be found in interior wood door specifications, particularly

those for projects seeking LEED certification. References to Underwriters' Laboratories (UL) testing may also found in the specifications for fire-rated doors. The specification may also refer to the WDMA (Window and Door Manufacturer's Association) *Technical Handbook*.

UL is an organization that tests products to determine whether they meet pre-established criteria. If the product passes the test, it often receives a label or certificate stating that it meets or exceeds the criteria.

AWI, WDMA, and TCNA (Tile Council of North America) are examples of architectural trade organizations. These groups are good sources of information about a particular product or type of construction; there are hundreds of trade organizations representing every building product imaginable. Most have a technical services section on their website with in-depth information about the product or method the group represents. Some of these groups publish handbooks of typical installation details, such as the TCNA *Handbook for Ceramic Tile Installation*, which is commonly referred to in specifications.

The FSC documents the chain of custody of wood products to prove that materials were grown and harvested in a sustainable way. This documentation can be necessary for projects seeking LEED certification.

CSI (Construction Specifications Institute) establishes standards used when organizing and writing specifications. Although these standards may be followed when preparing the specification, they would not be referred to in the document.

48. The answer is B.

The contract documents form the contractual relationship between the owner and contractor and are defined in Subparagraph 1.1.1 of AIA Document A201.

> The Contract Documents consist of the Agreement between the Owner and Contractor (hereinafter the Agreement), Conditions of the Contract (General, Supplementary and other Conditions), Drawings, Specifications, Addenda issued prior to execution of the Contract, other documents listed in the Agreement, and Modifications issued after execution of the Contract...

Modifications issued after execution of the contract can include change orders, construction change directives, a written amendment to the contract signed by both parties, or a written order for a minor change in the work issued by the architect.

Anything associated with bidding—including sample forms, the advertisement or invitation to bid, instructions to bidders, and the bid itself—is not a part of the contract documents. The contract documents represent the entire agreement between the owner and contractor, so anything that was negotiated or discussed prior to the agreement but not integrated into the written document is not a part of the contract.

49. The answer is B.

All of the floor space within a building can be classified into one of the following four categories.

- *net assignable area:* area that can be assigned to an occupant, including service and custodial spaces and restrooms

- *circulation area:* areas required for access to subdivisions of space such as stairwells, corridors, elevators, lobbies, and so on

- *mechanical area:* all mechanical spaces such as equipment rooms, duct shafts, boiler rooms, and so on

- *construction area:* area occupied by exterior walls, structural elements, and partitions

The *gross floor area* or architectural area of the building is equivalent to the sum of these four categories, plus any factored unenclosed or semi-enclosed areas. *Factored* means that the actual area of spaces such as canopies, balconies, pipe spaces less than 6 ft (1829) or terraces, is multiplied by a factor of 0.5 to arrive at a weighted number used in the tally.

50. The answer is D.

Life-cycle cost analysis allows designers and owners to evaluate the total cost of a product or system over its useful life. This facilitates an objective comparison between two or more options based upon a number of factors, including their initial purchase price, long-term maintenance costs, replacement costs over time, and any portion of the investment that may be recouped through salvage fees. Of course, this analysis is not the only factor that should be considered when making decisions about what to include in a building's design, but it does permit a comprehensive look at the total cost to the owner that decision will incur. An item that looks like a bargain in terms of its present-day purchase price may have steep operational costs or a short lifespan, requiring replacement in just a few years. Life-cycle costing takes all of these factors into consideration and converts all of the costs to present-day values so that they can be compared effectively.

51. The answer is B.

Bid amounts must be expressed on the bid form both in words and in numerical form. If there is a discrepancy between the two, the words prevail. The bid is valid and should be interpreted as $756,452.

52. The answer is B.

The American Institute of Architects published the first edition of the General Conditions (now AIA Document A201) in 1911. It grew from the Uniform Contract, published in 1888, which was the first agreement between owners and contractors to be used nationwide. The second edition of the General Conditions, published in 1915, was the result of reviews of the 1911 edition by architects and building contractors, and it better represented the interests of all three parties involved in a building project. In 1916, the AIA introduced the first Standard Form of Agreement Between Owner and Architect (now AIA Document B141).

53. The answer is B.

The most appropriate way to modify an AIA document is to attach supplementary conditions. AIA Document 511, *Guide for Supplementary Conditions*, suggests standard language for changes to the general conditions. The owner's attorney, not the architect, should write these conditions or any modifications if the document is an agreement between the owner and the contractor.

It is acceptable to strike out portions of the standard form of agreement or to add handwritten text, but only if all handwritten changes are initialed by the party to be bound. If handwritten modifications are made to the contract, the modifications may not render the original text illegible.

Retyping standard documents is a violation of copyright. In addition, one of the strengths of the AIA documents is that contractors are already familiar with the standard forms, and by reading the modifications they can understand quickly the unique requirements of a particular project. If the format and language of the document is revised, the contractor may determine it necessary to add fees to its bid to cover perceived risk.

Owners are not required to use AIA documents for construction contracts, and they have the right to have an attorney draft a new contract. However, an attorney who doesn't specialize in construction law may not understand conventional practices of the industry. Bids may be higher because contractors cannot rely on the "ground rules" they have come to expect. Architects should be extremely careful with contracts that are not based on the AIA documents, because they may require the architect to fulfill a role or accept responsibility that is not traditionally required, and for which the architect may not be insured. The architect's insurance carrier and/or attorney should always review owner-drafted contracts.

54. The answer is B.

Claims-made professional liability insurance policies require the policy to be in effect both at the time that the incident occurs and at the time that the claim is actually made. If a claim is made on a project that was completed a number of years earlier, the claim will only be covered if the architect is still insured under the same policy he or she held at the time services were rendered. This means that the architect cannot allow the policy to lapse, or past projects may not be covered. If a firm wishes to change insurance carriers and previously held a claims-made policy, the firm should investigate the purchase of *prior acts policies* to ensure that their previous work is adequately covered.

Accident- or *occurrence*-type policies will cover claims that are made for incidents that occurred when the policy was in effect, regardless of whether the policy is in effect at the time that the claim is made.

55. The answer is D.

A *pro forma* is an analysis of the costs and revenues projected for a potential project and should be a part of the owner's initial planning. Generally this is required to secure adequate funding for the project from lenders or investors.

56. The answer is A.

Most construction projects are bid as *stipulated sum* agreements; the contractor agrees to provide the work illustrated in the contract documents for a certain amount of money in a certain period of time, and the owner agrees to pay him the specified amount. If it actually costs more to build the project, the contractor has to absorb the loss. If it costs less, he gets to keep the extra money. The benefit to this type of contract is that all of the participants in the project know what the cost will be from the beginning.

However, owners may elect to use a *cost-plus-fee* contract for a number of reasons: If they have a hard and fast deadline that they must meet, if the scope of the work is unknown at the start of construction, or if the highest quality of construction is of critical importance, cost-plus-fee structures are often to the owner's benefit.

A *cost-plus agreement with a fee for overhead and profit based upon a percentage of construction cost* does little to motivate the contractor to be efficient. As the contractor sees it, the more time and money it takes to build the project, the greater his payment for overhead and profit. If he builds a project quickly and realizes savings for the owner, he does not get a cut of those savings.

However, a *cost-plus agreement with a fixed fee for overhead and profit* can encourage a contractor to be more efficient. It is particularly motivating if the owner offers a bonus for expeditious completion of the work. If the contractor can reduce costs to the owner and build the project quickly, he still receives the fixed amount of overhead and profit. The contractor may incur fewer administrative costs and therefore a larger share of the amount allocated for overhead becomes profit.

Unit costs are often a part of a contract when the exact amount of work cannot be determined at the time of contract negotiations.

57. The answer is D.

AIA Document A201 addresses subcontractors in Paragraph 5.2. The contractor is required to submit a list of proposed subcontractors to the architect and owner for review. If the architect and/or owner have objections to any of the proposed subcontractors, they must notify the contractor in writing. The contractor is responsible for proposing an alternate subcontractor. Assuming that the original proposed subcontractor was "reasonably capable" of performing the work, the contractor would be entitled to an adjustment of the contract sum or time to reflect the new subcontractor's price or schedule, which would be documented in a change order. After the list of subcontractors has been approved, the contractor may not make changes unless he obtains the permission of the owner and architect.

58. The answer is B.

Arbitration is binding on all parties and, under ordinary circumstances, the decisions of arbitrators may not be appealed. Arbitration is completely separate from the judicial system. In rare instances, the courts may be called upon to respond to a case where allegations of fraud or partiality are made against an arbitrator or where there is reason to believe that the arbitration board made a decision on an issue that was not included in the agreement to arbitrate. In most circumstances, however, arbitration and litigation are two very distinct paths of dispute resolution and they do not cross.

Arbitration is generally less expensive than litigation but more expensive than negotiation or mediation. If the parties have agreed to arbitrate, they must abide by the arbitrator's decision. Arbitration places the disagreement into the hands of an objective third party, usually someone familiar with the construction industry, to render a decision. Both parties receive a list of potential arbitrators and have the opportunity to strike the names of persons to whom they object. An arbitrator or arbitration board is selected from the names that remain, or, under the Uniform Arbitration Act, each party chooses one arbitrator and together the arbitrators select a third. The arbitrator hears the evidence from both parties and upon conclusion of the hearings issues a statement with the arbitrator's findings and the amount due to the prevailing party. The decision is final, and unless the parties request a "reasoned" award, no explanation is provided.

59. The answer is D.

Hatches are often used on architectural drawings to indicate materials used, rather than designating the materials with labels or notes. This graphic shorthand allows the drawings to be simpler and less cluttered with text. The material hatches shown in this question are those recommended by *Architectural Graphic Standards*.

60. The answer is D.

Local *zoning ordinances* address the relationship of structures to their sites, and building codes address methods and materials of construction permitted within sites. A zoning ordinance normally breaks a municipality into "zones" (commercial, residential, industrial, etc.) and defines where buildings may be constructed and how much building is permitted on a lot. Zoning ordinances can also address allowable uses, parking requirements, special requirements of historic districts or areas subject to a design or architectural review board, and site planning issues.

61. The answer is A.

Ideally, value engineering should be undertaken as early in the project as possible. In practice, however, it often occurs much later, giving it a bad reputation among architects for stripping all of the "good stuff" out of a design and requiring extensive (and expensive) revision of work that had been "complete."

Value engineering is a process that identifies areas of potential savings, analyzes their potential cost impact, and selects the preferred options. An informal form of value engineering can be completed in-house by the architect after an initial opinion of probable cost has been generated, and provides a good way for the architect to communicate to the owner that a design in the owner's best interest is being generated. Based upon this information, the architect and owner can make decisions and set priorities that reflect the goals of the project. Ideally, this analysis should be a standard part of every architectural project and should be ongoing as the architect makes choices about the optimal types of materials and construction methods for this particular building.

Often, a third-party value engineer is hired by the owner to determine appropriate methods of reducing cost. The value engineer may facilitate a workshop including representatives of the architect, owner, consultants, and cost estimators. The participants will evaluate the design and propose cost-saving methods. This can be very effective if it is done early in the design process, but the closer the project is to completion, the less advantageous the process will be for the owner. The changes suggested may have serious ramifications in other parts of the design, forcing the prices of those elements up. It is critical that the architect evaluate these late proposals very carefully. If elements from the proposal are to be incorporated into the design, the architect should pay special attention to other parts of the design that may be affected by the changes and carefully coordinate the construction documents to avoid errors or omissions.

62. The answer is A.

The U.S. National CAD Standard was developed to simplify and standardize the way that a set of documents is assembled and cross-referenced, with the intention of making it easier for someone unfamiliar with the documents to find information expeditiously. Each sheet is given a letter and number designation corresponding to the information that is located on the sheet.

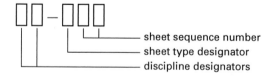

Architectural sheets are given the discipline designator of A. The second space for a discipline designator is often omitted but can be used to further define the discipline that developed the documents. Level 1 discipline designators are

G   general

H   hazardous materials

V   survey/mapping

B   geotechnical

W   civil works

C   civil

L   landscape

S   structural

A   architectural

I   interiors

Q   equipment

F   fire protection

P   plumbing

D   process

M   mechanical

E   electrical

T   telecommunications

R   resource

X   other disciplines

Z   contractor/shop drawings

O   operations

The sheet type designators are

0   schedules, master keynote legend, general notes

1   plans

2   elevations

3   sections

4   large-scale views

5   details

6   schedules and diagrams

7   user-defined

8   user-defined

9   three-dimensional representations

Each sheet is divided into a grid like a map, with numerical coordinates across the top of the sheet and alphabetical coordinates on the side. Title block information is located at the right side of the sheet in either a horizontal or vertical format. Each drawing is placed within the grid and referred to by its coordinates and sheet number. For example, a column detail may be placed in the lower right corner of one of the A-500 detail sheets; the marker on the plan sheet would refer to the detail as A-14/A-500, and the person reading the drawings would know exactly where to go to find that particular detail.

Another hallmark of the U.S. National CAD Standard system is the use of *keynotes*. Keynotes are abbreviations that may be coordinated with CSI MasterFormat divisions and that identify particular building elements in lieu of written notes. For example, fire-rated gypsum board may be designated "09 21 16.A." A keynote symbol would point to that element on the drawings, and a full definition of the material, such as "09 21 16.A—⅝ in fire-rated (type X) gypsum board" would be listed in a note block. The master list of keynotes for a project can be used as a checklist for preparing the specifications to ensure that all materials are properly defined.

Additional information on the U.S. National CAD Standard is available at www.nationalcadstandard.com.

63.   **The answer is B.**

The contractor should retrieve his bid from the owner, correct it, and resubmit it prior to the deadline for receipt of bids. This would be the best way to modify the price. The architect should not interfere with the bidding process by modifying the bid in any way.

64.   **The answer is B.**

An architect's interpretations of the contract documents are performed in a *quasi-judicial* capacity. AIA Document A201, Subparagraph 4.2.12, states

> Interpretations and decisions of the Architect will be consistent with the intent of and reasonably inferable from the Contract Documents… When making such interpretations and initial decisions, the Architect will endeavor to secure faithful performance by both Owner and Contractor, will not show partiality to either, and will not be liable for results of interpretations or decisions so rendered in good faith.

65.   **The answer is A.**

AIA Document A201, Paragraph 10.2, charges the contractor with responsibility for safety precautions and programs. Though the architect should bring obviously unsafe conditions to the contractor's attention, it is the contractor's responsibility to resolve those conditions.

Despite the best preventative measures, however, accidents can occur on construction sites, and it is important to obtain assistance for injured persons as quickly as possible. The architect should first activate the emergency medical services system by calling 911 and reporting the accident, or by asking another witness to do so. In the event of an emergency, the architect should do whatever is possible to safeguard human life.

The superintendent should be notified as soon as possible of the accident. Paragraph 10.6 of AIA Document A201 gives the contractor the authority to act to prevent threatened damage, injury, or loss of life.

When the emergency situation has been resolved, the architect should fully document the incident, noting the name of the worker and any available information about his or her condition, the names of any other witnesses, the time and location of the incident, conditions observed at the site, and any other pertinent information. If a camera is available, the architect should also take pictures. This is *not* an investigation, it is simply preparing documentation of what the architect witnessed.

66.   The answer is B.

Choice B is language excerpted from AIA Document G702, *Application and Certification for Payment*. The architect is stating to the owner that, in the architect's professional opinion and based upon the information available, the contractor has completed the percentage of work listed on the pay application and is due a payment in the amount specified.

An architect cannot and should not certify anything that is outside of his or her direct knowledge or control. For example, the architect does not know how much the contractor has spent and cannot assure that the contract documents or contractor's work are in full compliance with the codes because the codes are constantly changing and are sometimes at variance with each other. By signing such a statement, the architect is making an express warranty or guarantee (the same thing in the eyes of the law). An action such as this raises the standard of reasonable care required of the architect, which means that an architect is required to do what a reasonably prudent architect would do in the same community in the same time frame, given the same or similar facts and circumstances. While the law protects professionals who act reasonably and prudently and who use their best professional judgment, when a professional makes a guarantee or oversteps his boundaries, he may be held liable or negligent for his actions.

Clauses in the certification such as "to the best of the architect's knowledge, information, and belief," "based on the architect's observations and other information available to the architect," or "in the architect's professional opinion" help to qualify the statements and present them as accurate representations of the architect's perception of the situation, rather than a representation of the facts. Still, it is best not to certify information of which the architect does not have direct knowledge, for it puts the burden of responsibility for the accuracy of that information on the architect's shoulders.

67.   The answer is D.

There are two different issues related to the contractor's post-final-completion responsibilities to the owner addressed in AIA Document A201. The first is the *warranty* period established in Subparagraph 3.5.1. This section of the general conditions requires the contractor to warrant that the "work will be free from defects not inherent in the quality required or permitted, and that the work will conform to the requirements of the contract documents..." This warranty begins on the substantial completion date and continues through the period of the applicable statute of limitations or repose, whichever is shorter. The length of this period varies from state to state and can be anywhere from two to 12 years.

The second obligation the contractor has to the owner is the one-year *correction period* outlined in Subparagraph 12.2.2. The correction period and the warranty period run concurrently. Within the first year after substantial completion, the contractor must correct any work found not to be in accordance with the contract documents at no cost to the owner.

In this situation, the work is in compliance with the contract documents. The first question that should be investigated is whether a separate warranty was required for the roofing materials. Warranty requirements for individual materials or assemblies should be outlined in the product specifications. If the material failed within its warranty period, the roofing manufacturer may be responsible for the repair. However, if it is found that the architect incorrectly specified a product not suited for the environmental conditions at the site or for this particular application, the architect may be held responsible for the cost of the repair.

68.   The answer is D.

Subparagraph 1.3.9.2 of AIA Document B141 addresses the issue of reimbursable expenses. *Reimbursable expenses* are costs directly related to a project that are incurred by the architect and charged to the owner. They may not be a part of the architect's overhead costs. Reimbursable expenses can include travel, accommodations, and meals; reproductions and postage; overtime work (with prior owner authorization); additional insurance that the architect purchases specifically for this project or at the owner's request; renderings, models, and mock-ups; and fees for jurisdictional approvals.

Subparagraph 1.3.9.2 lists common reimbursable expenses, and Subparagraph 1.3.9.3 requires the architect to keep records of reimbursable expenses for the owner's review, if desired. Subparagraph 1.5.5 gives the architect and owner the opportunity to list other agreed-upon reimbursable expenses.

Usually, the architect includes a markup to reimbursable expenses to cover administrative expenses and the cost of advancing money on the owner's behalf. This multiplier is determined in Subparagraph 1.5.4. Many firms bill reimbursables at 110% of the cost to the architect, but this may vary depending on firm policies and specific owner-architect agreements.

69. The answer is B.

Vicarious liability is indirect liability imposed on a party resulting from the acts or omissions of another person for whom the party is responsible. Architects can encounter this situation when they hire consultants; the architect is liable for any errors or omissions on the consultant's documents. A firm may be held liable for the actions of its employees while performing tasks related to their employment, whether it be an error in a specification or drawing, or a traffic accident caused by the employee talking on a cell phone while en route to a job site.

In addition, a firm could be held liable for the actions of a moonlighting employee if that employee gives the client the impression that the firm is involved with the work (such as if the employee uses a firm title block on a drawing or sends a fax with a company cover sheet). To protect themselves from claims against their liability insurance policies, many firms have instituted "no moonlighting" policies or require prior approval from a supervisor.

70. The answer is C.

A historic preservation district is an example of *overlay zoning*. The primary zoning designation for the properties shown might be commercial, residential, or some category therein, but improvements to all of the properties within the shaded areas have been determined to be subject to the consideration of the Architectural Review Board.

A *planned unit development* is an area set aside for a specific use, such as a residential subdivision or a mix of commercial and residential uses. Planned unit developments often

have less stringent site requirements and review site plans on a case-by-case basis.

Cluster zoning allows structures to be grouped on one part of a site to preserve open space on other parts of the site. Generally site plans for cluster zoning areas are reviewed on a case-by-case basis.

Inclusionary zoning requires construction of low-income housing as a condition of approval.

71. The answer is C.

AIA Document A201, Paragraph 11.4, requires the owner to purchase and maintain builder's all-risk or equivalent insurance.

An *all-risk* insurance policy may not exclude any of the following.

- fire
- vandalism, malicious mischief, or riot
- explosion from all causes
- water damage
- testing and start-up
- mechanical or electrical breakdown
- theft
- collapse
- earthquakes, floods, or windstorms
- falsework
- temporary buildings
- debris removal, including demolition occasioned by enforcement of any applicable legal requirements

Some common exclusions include:

- war
- terrorism (although acts of terrorism that meet certain criteria are *not* excluded based upon the Terrorism Risk Insurance Act of 2002)
- nuclear hazards
- fraud by the insured
- employee theft
- inventory shortage or mysterious disappearance
- mold
- asbestos

72.   The answer is B.

Most fire deaths occur in single-family residences. Data from the National Fire Protection Association (NFPA) shows that approximately 2500 people have died in fires in single-family residences each year since 2000, and another 10,000 have been injured each year in such fires. During the same time period, an average of 100 people per year died in non-residential fires (excluding deaths attributed to terrorist acts on September 11, 2001), meaning that nearly 25 times more people are killed in fires in homes than in other locations.

A likely contributor to the problem is that single-family residences are the only types of buildings that do not currently require fire-suppression systems. The National Home Fire Sprinkler Coalition and NFPA advocate for mandatory installation of sprinkler systems in all single-family homes, but this is not yet a requirement of the International Residential Code.

73.   The answer is A.

Section 104 of the International Building Code outlines the duties and powers of the building official. This person is responsible for interpreting the code and inspecting projects for compliance with its policies and procedures. The final decision on matters of interpretation of code requirements is the building official's. In Paragraph 104.6, the code states that a building code representative may enter any structure or premises at any reasonable time if he believes that the building is noncompliant or presents a danger. In Paragraph 104.8, the building official is absolved of personal liability for decisions made in a professional capacity provided that those decisions are made "in good faith and without malice in the discharge of duties required by this code or other pertinent law or ordinance." Paragraph 110.1 states that no building may be occupied until the building official has issued a certificate of occupancy.

74.   The answer is A.

Inclement weather can have a significant impact on the amount of time it takes to erect a building. One way to minimize this affect is to construct portions of the building off-site and bring them to the site for installation. This allows work to continue indoors even when weather conditions prohibit progress.

Designs that contribute to improved sequencing can also help to reduce the amount of time necessary for construction. While the contractor is responsible for coordinating sequencing, architects can help make the project more efficient by developing details that allow certain trades to come on to the job site, complete their work, and leave before the next trade arrives. This simplifies scheduling for the general contractor and can result in cost savings for the owner and better construction details.

Use of union labor tends to lengthen the construction period. It would be impossible to choose a "best" time to begin construction, such as the spring, because inclement weather is unpredictable.

75.   The answer is 10 days.

Applications for payment must be submitted at least 10 days in advance of the payment date according to AIA Document A201, Subparagraph 9.3.1. The date of payment is established in the owner-contractor agreement, A101.

Subparagraph 9.4.1 states that the architect then has seven days to review the application and either certify it and send it to the owner for payment, or reject it and provide the reasons for the rejection to the contractor in writing.

76.   The answer is B.

Indicating that the items are to be furnished by the owner and installed by the contractor requires the contractor to be responsible for coordination and installation. *N.I.C.* means "not in contract" and the contractor has no responsibility for those items; they are indicated on the drawings for information only. *Cash allowances* are used when an owner wishes to include an item in the contract but has not yet selected something to be specified. If the items were noted by name, such as "range" or "refrigerator," it would imply that the contractor is responsible for providing, coordinating, and installing the equipment.

77.   The answer is D.

The administrative procedures for a project are established in Division 01 of the specifications, General Requirements. These sections explain exactly how the contractor is to fulfill the duties established in the general, supplementary, and special conditions.

The general, supplementary, and special conditions, in addition to the Owner-Contractor Agreement (AIA Document A101), establish the legal relationship between the two parties and define their rights. The architect's duties in administering the construction contract are also defined by these documents.

78. The answer is D.

Tolerance is the amount that an element of a building is permitted to be "off" from the specified dimension. Acceptable tolerances for building materials are dependent on their level of quality, their physical properties, the stage in the construction process during which they are to be installed, and the way the materials will be used. Two adjacent, different materials can both be within their acceptable tolerances and not align exactly. For these reasons, it is important the architect's drawings allow for some "play," or dimensional adjustment, and that tolerances specified by the architect agree with cited industry standards for that specific material. Architects should be aware that requiring exceptionally high levels of precision and low tolerances can cause construction costs to escalate; however, if such accuracy is critical to the project, these requirements must be specified.

Wood paneling would have the most restrictive tolerances, as even small deviations from the prescribed dimensions would be noticeable.

79. The answer is C.

AIA Document A201, Paragraph 3.10, requires the contractor to prepare and submit a construction schedule for the owner's and architect's information. Often, the General Requirements (Division 01 of the specifications) require a contractor to use the *critical path method* (CPM) of scheduling to develop this plan for the construction period. The use of the critical path method is not limited to construction projects and can be a good way to organize any complex undertaking, including scheduling the preparation of contract documents within an architectural firm.

Sequencing cannot be shown accurately on a bar chart. *Bar charts*, also known as *Gantt charts*, are best for evaluating duration only, because they list the activities to be completed but do not explain interrelationships between the tasks. (For example, a bar chart would not show that concrete foundations must be poured before wall framing begins.) A bar chart is usually structured so that the activities occurring first are at the top of the chart and subsequent activities are listed later.

Items on the critical path must be accomplished by the time they are scheduled to be complete, and they must be completed in the specified order, or project completion will be delayed. Critical path items are defined by their earliest or latest possible start and finish dates and the duration of the activities. Not all construction activities listed in the schedule will be on the critical path.

Contractors prefer to have the duration of activities be within one payment period. This makes it easy to show the owner what has and has not been accomplished to date and simplifies preparing the application for payment. It is also advantageous to the contractor to keep the schedule up to date throughout the project to provide back-up for claims for extension of the contract time due to owner changes or other conditions such as inclement weather.

Float is the period of time between the end of an activity and the project completion date. Activities with float can be started or finished within a range of time prior to the project completion date, and they will not affect the completion of the project as long as these activities are completed before a subsequent activity. There is no float on the critical path.

80. The answer is C.

Force majeure means "greater force" and is used to describe situations where damages or delays are caused by forces beyond the control of either party to a contract. AIA Document A201, Paragraph 8.3.1, Delays and Extensions of Time, allows the contractor to request an extension of the contract time due to "unavoidable casualties or other causes beyond the Contractor's control." The contractor must initiate any claims within 21 days of the event per Subparagraph 4.3.2. The contract is then modified by a change order or construction change directive issued by the architect.

Examples of acts that may excuse performance under a force majeure clause are natural disasters, acts of war, terrorist attacks, and labor disputes such as union strikes.

81. The answer is C.

The indemnification provision, Paragraph 3.18 of AIA Document A201, requires the contractor to indemnify the owner, architect, architect's consultants, and any agents or employees of those parties from

> …claims, damages, losses and expenses… attributable to bodily injury, sickness, disease or death, or to injury to or destruction of tangible property (other than the Work itself), but only to the extent caused by the negligent acts or omissions of the Contractor, a Subcontractor, anyone directly or indirectly employed by them or anyone for whose acts they may be liable.

This provision specifically excludes claims that are covered by project management protective liability insurance. Many of these types of claims would be covered by this policy if it is in effect on a project. This part of the general conditions should be carefully reviewed by the owner's legal counsel, as indemnification statues vary by jurisdiction.

82.   The answer is B.

AIA Document B141 does not require the owner to provide evidence that he or she has secured adequate funding for the project. It does, however, require the owner to determine a budget for the cost of the work and for the project. The project budget includes the architect's compensation. The contract also requires the owner to provide a program and schedule. The architect must compare the budget, program, and schedule to determine if the requirements can be satisfied given the amount the owner plans to spend. If it is not possible, the architect should notify the owner of adjustments that will need to be made to any of the three components (time, cost, and quality) or of the consultant services that will be required. This responsibility is detailed in Article 2.3, Evaluation and Planning Services.

The architect is obligated to work within the owner's budget per Paragraph 2.1.7. It is important to understand the scope of the work from the beginning and make this first check to assure that both parties have a similar understanding of the project's feasibility.

83.   The answer is D.

Modifying work prepared by another designer can be a sticky situation. Whether an architect decides to accept this job depends on many factors. The architect may decline the job if it seems too complicated to deal with the issues of permission and copyright in comparison to the projected fee. The requirements of the NCARB Rules of Conduct are explicit regarding the need to obtain proper permissions and honor copyright, and both may be very difficult to do in a situation such as this. The cost of the time and legwork it will take to "cover all the bases" and the potential risk and liability that this project may bring with it may be enough for the architect to decide to reject it.

The architect may advise the owner to contact the original author of the drawings to prepare the revisions, or may refer the owner to a home designer who is not a licensed architect to prepare the drawings in jurisdictions where an architect is not required for residential work. If the home designer pursues the project, permission from the original author must be obtained.

If the firm chooses to accept the project, the architect must first obtain permission from the original designer to use and modify the drawings and CAD files. The NCARB Rules of Conduct require an architect to conduct a thorough review of the work so that he or she understands and can support the design decisions the previous designer made. See Rule 5: Professional Conduct for further information on the requirements. The architect may also wish to consult an intellectual property attorney to confirm that proper permission to modify the work has been obtained.

84.   The answer is A.

Architect's supplemental instructions (or ASIs) allow the architect to clarify information in the construction documents or make minor changes to the work, provided that those changes do not affect the contract sum or time. This authority is provided by Paragraph 7.4.1 of AIA Document A201.

85.   The answer is D.

It is the contractor's responsibility to notify the surety of any change orders issued during a project so that the amount of insurance coverage may be increased or decreased as necessary.

A *clerk of the works* is a representative hired by the owner to monitor progress on-site and keep project records. The architect's project representative is an employee of the architect who is on-site whenever construction is underway. This full-time representation is referenced in Subparagraphs 1.4.1.3 and 2.8.3 of AIA Document B141, and is contracted separately using AIA Document B352, *Duties, Responsibilities and Limitations of Authority of the Architect's Project Representative*.

If a contractor discovers an error in the documents, it is the architect's responsibility to correct the error at no cost; however, the architect is not responsible for the cost of construction to correct the error unless it can be proven that the architect was negligent.

According to AIA Document A201, Paragraph 7.3, Construction Change Directives, only the owner and architect's signatures are required on a construction change directive for it to be valid.

86.   The answer is B.

An architect is not qualified to give a client advice regarding bonds and insurance. However, since architects often have a good deal more experience with construction than many owners, clients often ask architects for assistance with these requirements. Architects may give their clients AIA Document G612, *Owner's Instructions Regarding the Construction Contract, Insurance and Bonds, and Bidding*, to help explain the types of insurance available and provide a worksheet for defining the owner's requirements. Architects may also assist the owner's insurance agent; however, the final advice regarding insurance should come from the agent and be based on the agent's professional knowledge, not the architect's.

87. The answer is B.

Although both the owner and the contractor are contractually required to carry insurance relative to a project, only the contractor is required to provide certificates of insurance per AIA Document A201, Subparagraph 11.1.3. One of the most popular forms used to prepare this documentation is the ACORD Certificate of Insurance. ACORD, which stands for Association for Cooperative Operations Research and Development, is a nonprofit organization that develops standards for the insurance and financial services industries. If this document is used, it should be accompanied by AIA Document G715, *Supplemental Attachment for ACORD Certificate of Insurance*, which provides instructions for completing the ACORD form and contains additional space for information required by the construction contract that is not called for on the form.

The owner is required by Subparagraph 11.4.6 to file copies of required insurance policies with the contractor before any exposure to loss may occur.

All required insurance provisions mandate that one party give the other 30 days notice before any insurance is cancelled. This gives the other party time to consider the option of continuing the policy.

The architect and subcontractor are not parties to the owner-contractor agreement and are not required by this contract to carry insurance. However, insurance requirements may be detailed in their agreements with the owner or contractor, respectively.

88. The answer is B.

In the *schematic design* phase, the architect works with the owner to determine the requirements of the project and complete preliminary sketches to work through the relationships of spaces and masses. When a preliminary design is agreed upon, the architect completes a preliminary cost estimate based upon a cost per square foot or cost per unit structure.

Programming is the process of developing a written description of project objectives, space requirements, existing site conditions or constraints, and special requirements for a building.

In *design development*, the architect further refines the concepts explored in schematic design. The architect then prepares the drawings and specifications for the project during the *construction documents* phase.

89. The answer is B.

The joinder provisions in AIA Documents A201, Subparagraph 4.6.4, and B141, Subparagraph 1.3.5.4, restrict arbitration to the parties joined by the contract, unless the parties (architect, owner, contractor, and any other entity to be joined in the case of the owner-contractor agreement; architect, owner, and any other entity to be joined in the case of the owner-architect agreement) agree in writing to consolidate arbitrations regarding one specific issue. This language is found in all AIA documents that require arbitration, because the architect and contractor are held to different standards of performance. It is simpler (and less costly) for arbitrators to render a decision when there are only two parties and when a single standard of performance is in question rather than to determine responsibility in a multiparty hearing.

In a case where all three parties are involved in the dispute, two arbitrations should be held: one for the owner and architect, and one for the owner and contractor. The contractor and architect would never be in arbitration because they do not have a contractual relationship. However, one or the other could be called as a witness in either hearing.

90. The answer is B.

Depending on the situation, it could be appropriate to do any or all of the things listed prior to certifying a pay application that includes stored materials. In certifying applications for payment, it is the architect's responsibility to protect the interests of the owner. The architect should do whatever is necessary to determine that the materials are in the possession of the contractor and are being stored properly before consenting to payment for the windows. In most cases, requesting a copy of the bill of sale and verifying that the items are indeed in the contractor's possession and are being stored appropriately would be adequate documentation to certify the pay application.

When an owner is willing to pay for materials stored off site, the situation should be addressed in the supplementary conditions, which should define where the materials are to be stored, what type of insurance is required, and how the materials will be transported to the site. Each time the contractor submits a pay application that includes a request for payment for stored materials, he or she should also submit supporting documentation, such as a bill of sale and evidence of insurance coverage. If the supporting documents are not submitted with the application for payment, the architect may request them from the contractor. The architect should also visit the site where the materials are being stored to verify that they are at the specified location and that the contractor is adhering to the security precautions defined in the supplementary conditions.

If there is any question or concern about the appropriateness of the documents or the provisions for protecting the owner's interest in the materials, those concerns should be referred to the owner's attorney for evaluation. In a situation such as this, the architect may also wish to obtain written approval from the owner prior to certifying the application for payment.

91.   The answer is B.

Certain terms can be misinterpreted and can commit the architect to a higher standard of care than would normally be expected of a professional.

The word "supervision" should never be used to describe an architect's duties during construction administration. Legal interpretations of the term have held that it means that the architect has a right to "manage, direct, and control" and therefore takes responsibility for the way that the work is performed. In the context of a construction project, this is the contractor's responsibility, and the architect should not say or do anything to confuse the roles defined in the contract.

It is impossible to record every existing condition in a building, and the term "as-built" drawings may lead someone looking at the documents to believe that the drawings are more accurate than they really are. It is more appropriate to refer to these as *record drawings*, or documents that show the existing conditions in a building to the best of the preparer's ability. Record drawings are often based upon a marked up set of documents complied by the contractor during the course of the project or can be prepared by an architect based upon field verification.

It is an architect's responsibility to certify pay applications. However, if asked to certify other documents, the architect should carefully verify that the language of the document is not in conflict with the professional standard of care. (See the solution to Prob. 66 for additional information on certification.)

It is acceptable to use the term "periodic" to describe site visits that occur on a regular basis, such as a Monday morning meeting at the construction site each week. However, the owner-architect agreement only requires site visits at "intervals appropriate to the stage of construction," and the timing of those visits is at the discretion of the architect. If construction meetings are to be held on a regular basis, the owner-architect agreement should include provisions to compensate the architect for attending and for preparing documentation of the meeting, if applicable.

92.   The answer is C.

Sunk costs are expenses that have been incurred on a project prior to the baseline date and cannot be recovered. Generally these costs are disregarded when analyzing life-cycle costs, because it is impossible to make decisions about the best way to spend money that has already been spent. Sunk costs are incorporated into analyses of total project costs.

93.   The answer is D.

A mechanic's lien gives a contractor, subcontractor, or material supplier the right to place a claim against an owner's property if proper payment for materials or services has not been provided. (In some states, an architect can also file a lien if the firm has not been paid for professional services rendered.) A lien encumbers the title to a property and can force an owner to sell it to pay the company providing materials or services. The claim is relevant only to the project, not the owner's other assets.

A contractor is required to submit evidence that the work is free of liens before receiving payments per AIA Document A201, Subparagraphs 9.3.3 and 9.10.2. The contractor may also be required to submit AIA Document G706, *Contractor's Affidavit of Payment of Debts and Claims*, and/or AIA Document G706A, *Contractor's Affidavit of Release of Liens*, to ensure that the owner will have clear title to the property upon final payment.

Liens are not permitted on publicly owned projects; bonds are used instead.

94.   The answer is D.

AIA Document C141, *Standard Form of Agreement Between Architect and Consultant*, may be used to form the contractual relationship between the architect and a consultant. It is most often used for consulting engineers but can also be used for relationships with consultants in other disciplines, such as interior designers or specialty consultants. This document is coordinated with AIA Documents B141 and A201. Document C141 requires the consultant to prepare and coordinate the work relevant to the project, prepare cost estimates for the work and design within the budgetary guidelines established by the owner, and assist the architect with the preparation of the contract documents, bidding, and construction administration responsibilities.

95. The answer is B.

Project records should be kept until the end of the statute of repose period. The AIA Best Practices advise keeping them for one year past the longest applicable date and then destroying them. Exceptions to the guideline include projects with design or financial problems or projects in which new types of construction were employed. Some firms choose to archive these projects indefinitely to permit easy access to the records necessary to construct a defense in a potential lawsuit.

Archived project records should include

- contracts, correspondence related to those contracts, and any modifications, such as addenda, change orders, and construction change directives

- design criteria as approved by the owner

- research findings, calculations, and other evidence of due diligence on the part of the architect and consultants

- records of telephone conversations, meeting minutes, and other project correspondence

- copies of the drawings and specifications

- submittal logs, site visit reports, and correspondence with the contractor, such as requests for information

- closeout documentation

96. The answer is A.

Contract time is measured in calendar days. The target date for substantial completion would be May 13, because it is 60 days from the date of commencement. No exceptions are made for weekends or holidays when calculating contract time.

97. The answer is D.

A *wythe* is a continuous vertical section of a brick wall. Often, two or more wythes of brick are placed parallel to one another with an air space in between and are tied together with metal ties or reinforcement to form a *cavity wall*. Traditionally, bricks were turned perpendicular to the stretchers (placed in the header position) to lock the wythes together. If the space in between is filled with reinforcing bars and mortar, it is called a *reinforced grouted wall*. A single wythe of brick can also be used as a *veneer* on the exterior of a wood or metal stud or concrete masonry unit wall.

98. The answer is C.

AIA Document B141, Subparagraph 2.1.7.4, allows a 90-day grace period from the time that the construction documents are submitted to the owner. Delaying bidding can have a significant impact on construction prices. Given the volatility of the construction marketplace, even a 90-day grace period may be too long to insure that the prices used by bidders will be consistent with the prices used in estimating, especially for materials with great fluctuations in price, such as glass and steel.

99. The answer is A.

The *design-build* approach to project delivery allows an owner to contract with one entity who agrees to provide both design and construction services. This entity can be a construction company with in-house designers, an architect and contractor approaching the project as a team, or a construction manager who subcontracts both design and construction. As a result of skipping the bidding phase, the overall time required for the project is shortened. With only one entity to deal with, contract administration is simplified. The owner also has more accurate cost information available early in the process.

However, in exchange for speed and simplicity, the owner often sacrifices control over the design and the materials and methods of construction. This approach requires that the owner have a well-defined program or list of criteria that the project must fulfill, and great confidence that the designer/builder will give a fair deal, because eliminating bidding eliminates the opportunity for the owner to compare prices. The design-build approach tends to work best for owners with previous construction project experience and very clearly defined needs.

100. The answer is B.

The owner is responsible for paying for uncovering and rebuilding the wall. Presumably, the architect requested that the drywall be removed because there was a reason to suspect that the construction was in error and the architect was protecting the owner's interests.

If the blocking had been in the wrong location, the contractor would be responsible for the cost of uncovering and repairing the work.

PRACTICE EXAM: VIGNETTE SOLUTIONS

BUILDING SECTION: PASSING SOLUTION

This vignette requires that the examinee draw a vertical section of a two-story building based on information shown in floor plans and the program requirements.

Solving Approach

Step 1 Draw the grade line. The grade line should be drawn near the section cut line to make it easier to see the relationship between the developing section and the existing floor plans without having to scroll the screen or constantly zoom in and out.

Step 2 Draw the exterior walls, carefully aligning them with the walls in the plans. The top of the walls can be left at an approximate height and adjusted later when the roof deck is established. Draw the interior bearing wall.

Step 3 Draw the slab on grade. (The slab sits on top of the grade line.)

Step 4 Draw the foundations under the bearing walls. The top of the foundation for the interior wall should be drawn directly beneath the slab on grade. The top of the spread footing should be drawn at the frost depth stated in the program, to allow a margin of error, as the bottom must be no higher than the frost depth.

Step 5 Draw a sketch line or circle to establish the first-floor ceiling height and the ceiling height for the higher space.

Step 6 Draw the ceilings for the first-floor ceiling and the high space.

Step 7 Draw sketch lines or circles to allow for the required clearance space above the ceiling for the light fixtures. On the actual exam, zoom in to do this.

Step 8 Draw the largest ducts required in the ceiling spaces of the high space and the lower, first-floor ceiling. Then, draw any remaining smaller ducts, aligning the tops of the smaller ducts with the largest ducts.

Step 9 Draw joists with their lower edges along the top of the ducts. Make sure to use the depth and spacing of the joists as shown at the section cut line and either a section or elevation view as indicated on the plans. Draw a 4 in (100) slab on top of the joists.

Step 10 Repeat steps 5 through 9 for the second-floor ceiling, light fixture space, ducts, and structure.

Step 11 Draw the interior partitions. Draw interior fire-rated partitions for any 1-hour rated partitions and draw interior partitions to the underside of the ceiling for other nonrated partitions. On the actual exam, there are separate draw tools for these two different partition types.

Step 12 Draw a sketch line or circle above the roof slabs at the required parapet height. Adjust the height of the top of the bearing walls as required.

Step 13 Double-check all elements and dimensions. On the actual exam, zoom in to do this. Make sure all the elements drawn are indicated at the section cut line and not where the grade line was drawn.

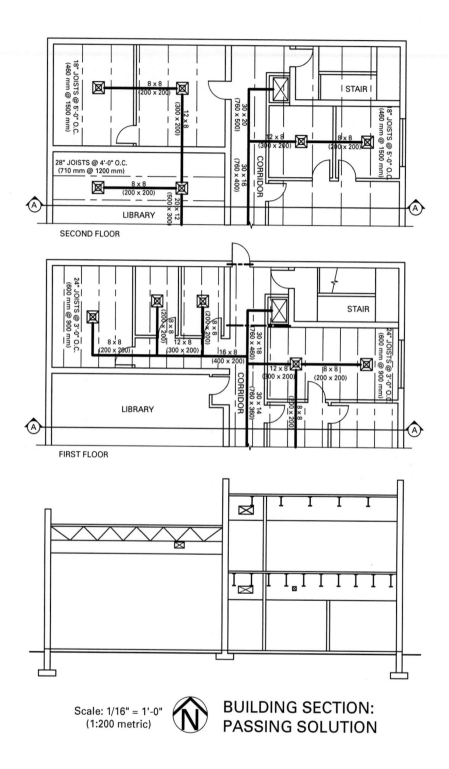

SECOND FLOOR

FIRST FLOOR

Scale: 1/16" = 1'-0"
(1:200 metric)

**BUILDING SECTION:
PASSING SOLUTION**

BUILDING SECTION:
FAILING SOLUTION

Pitfalls

Note 1   The interior partition on the first floor has not been indicated.

Note 2   The fire-rated partition has not been drawn to the underside of the roof slab.

Note 3   The second-floor roof joists are incorrectly drawn at 3 ft 0 in (915) on center and do not line up with the plan view.

Note 4   There is not enough space for the light fixtures above the library ceiling.

PROFESSIONAL PUBLICATIONS, INC.

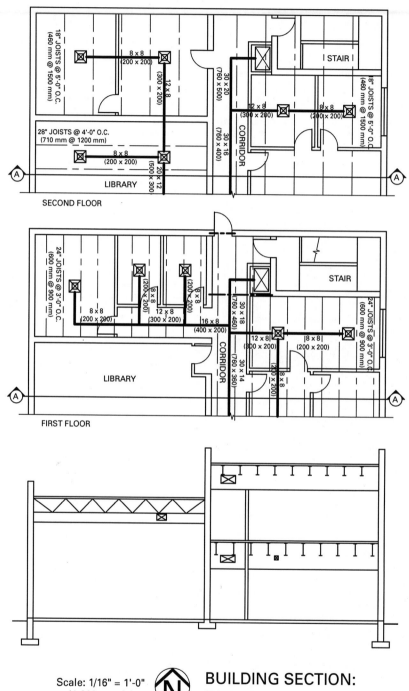

Scale: 1/16" = 1'-0"
(1:200 metric)

**BUILDING SECTION:
FAILING SOLUTION**